Routledge Revivals

Turkey

First published in 1985, this study, focusing on Turkey, looks at the underlying reasons why certain political, economic and social events have taken place in the country's history. It provides vital analysis of the political and economic issues of the country, and those that have affected it, as well as providing statistical material on all the key data of the political economy.

The book was originally published as part of the Middle East Research Institute (MERI) Reports on the Middle East which quickly established themselves as the most authoritative and up-to-date information on the state of affairs in the region.

Turkey

MERI Report

Middle East Research Institute

Routledge
Taylor & Francis Group

First published in 1985
by Croom Helm

This edition first published in 2015 by Routledge
2 Park Square, Milton Park, Abingdon, Oxon, OX14 4RN
and by Routledge
711 Third Avenue, New York, NY 10017

Routledge is an imprint of the Taylor & Francis Group, an informa business

Publisher's Note
The publisher has gone to great lengths to ensure the quality of this reprint but points out that some imperfections in the original copies may be apparent.

Disclaimer
The publisher has made every effort to trace copyright holders and welcomes correspondence from those they have been unable to contact.

A Library of Congress record exists under LC control number: 84028554

ISBN 13: 978-1-138-90211-4 (hbk)
ISBN 13: 978-1-315-69756-7 (ebk)
ISBN 13: 978-1-138-90226-8 (pbk)

MERI REPORT

TURKEY

Middle East Research Institute
University of Pennsylvania

CROOM HELM
London • Sydney • Dover, New Hampshire

Croom Helm Ltd, Provident House, Burrell Row,
Beckenham, Kent BR3 1 AT

Croom Helm Australia Pty Ltd, First Floor,
139 King Street, Sydney, NSW 2001, Australia

British Library Cataloguing in Publication Data

Turkey. – (Meri report)
1. Turkey – Social conditions –1960-
I. University of Pennsylvania. *Middle East Research Institute* II. Series
956.1'038 HN656.5.A8

ISBN 0-7099-3549-8

Croom Helm, 51 Washington Street, Dover,
New Hampshire 03820, USA

Library of Congress Cataloging in Publication Data

University of Pennsylvannia. Middle East Research Institute.
MERI report, Turkey.

1. Turkey – Politics and government – 1960-
2. Turkey – Foreign relations – 1960- . 3. Turkey – Economic conditions – 1960- . I. Title. II. Title: M.E.R.I. report, Turkey.
DR593.U54 1985 330.9561'038 84-28554
ISBN 0-7099-3549-8 (pbk.)

Printed and bound in Great Britain by
Antony Rowe Ltd., Chippenham

TABLE OF CONTENTS

I. Background

II. Political Analysis

Demography

Economy

Energy

Industry

I. BACKGROUND

1. **GEOGRAPHY.** Turkey is situated at the junction of Europe and Asia. This location on two continents has been a central feature of Turkish history, culture and politics. The country shares common borders with Greece and Bulgaria in the northwest, with the USSR and Iran in the east, and with Iraq and Syria in the south. It is bounded to the north by the Black Sea, to the west by the Aegean Sea, and to the south by the Mediterranean Sea. The Turkish Straits – the Bosphorus, the Sea of Marmara, and the Dardenelles – connect the Black Sea with the Aegean.

The area of Turkey is about 780,000 sq km (1 sq km = 0.386 sq mi), three times the size of the Federal Republic of Germany or slightly larger than Texas. The European part of the country is called Thrace (23,912 sq km), the larger Asian part, Anatolia. The country's total land frontiers extend over 2,625 km (1 km = 0.62 mi), while the length of the coastline is 7,110 km. The Tigris and Euphrates Rivers rise in eastern Turkey and flow southward to the Persian Gulf through Syria and Iraq. The largest river entirely within Turkey is the Kizilirmak, which flows northward from Sivas past Ankara (the capital city) to the Black Sea. Other major rivers include the Simav Cayi, feeding the Sea of Marmora, the Coruh, Yesil Izmak and Dakarya, discharging into the Black Sea, the Maritsa, flowing into the Aegean Sea, the Gedez, which drains into the Gulf of Izmir, and the Buyuk Mederes. Most rivers are unnavigable.

Turkey's topography is extremely varied. Its European region is an extension of the Balkan steppe of well-watered, gently rolling terrain dipping into the Sea of Marmara. To the East, Asiatic Turkey rises gradually into a high plateau. This semi-arid upland is cut off from the Black Sea by the Pontus Mountains in the north and from the Mediterranean Sea by the Taurus and Anti-Taurus mountains in the south. Further east, where the increasingly rugged countryside is dominated by Mt. Ararat with an elevation of 5,165 m (1 m = 3.28 ft), the Anatolian Plateau runs into the Caucasus range without encountering a natural frontier.

2. CLIMATE. The southern coastal plain is semi-tropical, with rainfall sufficient for citrus fruits and bananas. The average annual temperature is between 18-20° C (66-70° F). The Aegean coast enjoys hot, dry summers and mild winters, during which the average temperature falls to 14-15° C (58-60° F). Slightly cooler temperatures prevail along the Black Sea coast. The interior plateau has warm, dry summers, which become progressively shorter as one moves to the east. Winters are cool, and snow may persist from November into March near the Soviet border. East Anatolia and the interior parts of Turkey are subject to cold winters because they are shielded from the moderating effects of the sea breezes by the coastline mountains. The average temperatures over these areas are between -10 and 0° C in the winter (24-32° F). Rainfall is remarkably variable. Along the eastern Black Sea coast, towards the Soviet frontier, over 2,500 mm fall annually; elsewhere, amounts are very much smaller. Parts of the central plateau, being shut off by mountains from the influence of sea winds, are arid, with annual totals of under 250 mm and frequent expanses of salt steppe and desert. Precipitation, which comes for the most part in the winter, is adequate for cereal farming in the western part of the plateau.

3. POPULATION. Turkey's population was about 46,312,000 and the number of inhabitants per sq km was 59 in 1982. The annual average rate of increase of population was 2.3 percent during the period 1975-1980. The birth rate was 34.88 per 1,000, while the death rate was 9.99 per 1,000. The growth rate has been decreasing slowly since 1960.

It is estimated that 49.62 percent of the population is under 20, the median age being 20.19. In 1982, 37.9 percent of the population was under 15, 57.4 percent was between 15 and 64, and 6.4 was aged 65 or over. During the period 1975-80, life expectancy at birth was 58.3 for males and 62.8 for females. The infant mortality rate was 110.0 per 1,000.

Among the principal minority groups are the Kurds of the south-eastern portion of the country. The language spoken by the estimated 3 to 8 million Kurds is Kurdish, especially next to the Syrian and Iraqi borders. There are other groups of ethnic minorities. The Caucasians, Circassians and Georgians are found mainly in the north-east. There used to be large numbers of Greeks and Armenians throughout Turkey, but as a result of the deportations that started in the 1920s, the only place one may hear either language is in the city of Istanbul, where there are large numbers of both ethnic groups. Throughout the rest of the country, the official and most widely spoken language is Turkish.

The crude birth rate is expected to decline to 30.6 per 1,000 for the period 1980-1985, and the crude death rate likewise to 9.0 per 1,000. Infant mortality should decline substantially to 83.2 per 1,000, and life expectancy should rise to 60.6 for males and 65.5 for females.

4. RESOURCES. Turkey's principal human and natural economic potential is still relatively unexploited. Turkey has most of the natural resources to support rapid economic development. At the most basic level, the country has the fertile land and rainfall for a strong agricultural sector. Nearly 25 million ha, or about one-third of total land area, are under cultivation. About one-half of the cultivated area is devoted to cereals, of which the most important is wheat. With the introduction of high-yield strains of wheat in the 1960s, Turkey now produces a regular surplus of food. It has coal to supply its three steel mills, but lacks enough high-grade iron ore for their efficient operation. While low-grade coal and lignite is produced in quantities that meet domestic needs, Turkey's main energy deficiency is in oil; about eighty percent of the petroleum needed must be imported. Turkey has a good supply of most other minerals; in particular, it is a major source of chrome. Hydroelectric generation of electricity has already been extensively developed and no longer has the potential to meet Turkey's burgeoning power requirements. The new Turkish economic program applied since January 1980 explicitly recognized the waste of resources resulting from past policies and has attempted to correct those mistakes.

5. SOCIAL STRUCTURE. Turkey is rapidly becoming urban. Over 80 percent of the population 80 percent was rural just three decades ago; now only 55.8 percent of the population lives in the rural areas. Istanbul (4,871,000 in 1980) is the largest city and the strongest magnet for migrants. The capital Ankara (about 3.2 million), comes next, followed by Izmir, Adana, and Bursa. About 98 percent of the population is Muslim. Today nearly two million Turks are living in Western Europe, where they are employed mainly as miners, automobile workers, and in other heavy industries. Since the European economy no longer needs as many Turkish workers, the number in Europe, particularly in West Germany, has begun to decline. However, tens of thousands of Turks have gone to the Middle East, for the most part as construction workers in Libya, Iraq, and Saudi Arabia.

The division between rural and urban dwellers remains the most prominent social characteristic of the Turkish population. Dress, education, outlook, and wealth separate the traditional, underdeveloped, and generally impoverished rural inhabitants from the growing urban population. Cities are the home of Turkey's western-educated, modern elite who staff the government and provide its direction and cohesion. The city dwellers look down on their provincial compatriots who are engaged mainly in agriculture. Residents of the squatter settlements, who are the newest migrants to the cities form an intermediate group; they still maintain ties to the village, but increasingly adopt city ways.

Urban, educated women have achieved impressive access to professional life. Economic necessity and increasing educational levels combine to propel many women into careers. In government, the professions, and in the educational institutions, they have risen to important positions. Business and politics have been less welcoming environments. In the rural areas and among the less well educated in the cities, women are subject to the traditional constraints of conservative Islamic society. The home and farming tasks remain the focus of their activity. While social customs seek to isolate these women from contact with men to whom they are not related, the population shifts are increasingly bringing even the females in traditional roles into the mainstream of Turkish life.

6. RELIGION. Ataturk's efforts to separate religion and the state as well as to deemphasize Islamic traditions were quite successful. Although Islam was stated to be the official religion in the constitution of 1924, an amendment in 1928 removed this privilege. After 1950 subsequent governments have tried to re-establish links between religion and state affairs, but secularity has been protected by the revolution of 1960, the 1980 coup and the new 1982 constitution. However, in the past decade, minor parties sought to gain votes by claiming to represent religious interests. The National Salvation Party, with its frank appeal to the "prayer-rug" vote, achieved a significant swing position between the two major parties in the 1970s. As the decade progressed, however, its strength declined from a high point of 12 percent of the electorate. This result indicated that blatant manipulation of religious sentiment had a limited constituency.

7. POLITICAL STRUCTURE AND LEADERSHIP. The Turkish Armed Forces, headed by Chief of Staff General Kenan Evren, took over the administration of the country on September 12, 1980. Before that time, the normal political pattern had been one of vigorous competition between parties in a parliamentary structure under a constitution. This structure, however, fell apart in the late 1970s as the civilian governments became weaker and more and more fractured. Successive governments failed to arrest the rising wave of terrorism as unrest and anarchy increased. The military stepped in, repressed the terrorist movements and closed down all the political parties; at the same time a new quasi-presidential constitution, new political parties and electoral laws were brought into existence. All former politicians who held prominent positions were disqualified from political activity by the military government. Only new politicians were permitted to form new parties beginning April 25, 1983. Since that time, Turkey's political structure has been in transition. The new constitution, ratified by 91 percent of the voters in a nationwide referendum in November 1982, has redirected the system of checks and balances in the interests of fostering strong government.

Only three parties (17 were vetoed) were allowed to take part in the elections of 1983. The Nationalist Democracy Party (NDP), which was given the complete stamp of approval by the military government, was led by a retired general, Turgut Sunalp, whose main campaign position was anti-communism. The center-right Motherland Party (MP) was led by Turgut Ozal, the deputy prime minister responsible for economic affairs until July 1982. The Populist Party (PP) was led by Necdet Calp, an undersecretary at the prime minister's office until April 11, 1983. The new political parties, as artificial creations, however, failed to generate much excitement. In November 1983, Turkish voters decided that they did not want a continuation of the September 12 regime. Ozal, able to use public sentiment against the heavy-handed nature of the military government, was elected prime minister.

Ozal is identified by many with the middle class, whose support he successfully sought in the 1983 elections. His reforms have so far tended to favor the middle class: he moved to tax luxury consumption, increase credit to farmers and artisans, and reduce taxes on savings. He seems to have the cautious support of business circles, whose primary concerns are that he prove able to maintain order, and that his economic reforms prove effective in stimulating the economy and facing the challenges of the eighties.

8. MILITARY. The Turkish military is a functioning part of the NATO defense establishment. The Turkish Army has approximately 570,000 soldiers, 489,000 of whom are conscripts. Seven hundred thousand men are in the Reserves. The Navy, including marines, numbers 46,000 (36,000 conscripts). There are 70,000 Naval Reserves and five Naval bases. There are 53,000 men in the Turkish Air Force (33,000 conscripts). Reserves number 66,000. The Para-Military Forces (Gendarmerie) number 125,000.

U.S. military credit sales to Turkey in 1980 amounted to $208.3 million, while total Turkish military expenditures in 1982 came to $2.3 billion. There are three U.S. air bases in Turkey: Incirilik, Ankara and Karamursel.

9. FOREIGN RELATIONS. Since World War II, Turkey has aligned itself rather closely with the western bloc, whose primary objective has been the checking of Soviet expansionism. Turkey, as part of NATO, has attempted to play the part of a good and loyal ally. As a result Turkey's armed forces underwent great modernization; they were, however, placed under NATO command and not at the disposal of the Turkish government for any non-NATO purpose.

Turkey was, until the 1970s, isolating itself from its neighbors and most members of the developing world because of its strong ties to the United States and western Europe. More recently, however, Turkey has acted to pursue more independent policies. While not abandoning its westward orientation, Turkey has recently shown an interest in developing relations with the Islamic and Arab worlds, both politically and economically. This is reflected in the fact that Iran and Iraq are two of Turkey's main trading partners. Turkey also has economic ties with Libya, illustrating its turn toward the Islamic world.

10. ECONOMIC STRUCTURE. The agricultural sector has declined in relative importance. While it continues to employ a large percentage of the population, it has consistently been the sector with the lowest labor productivity. The industrial and the service and construction sectors, in which labor has been more productive, have grown considerably in recent years.

The agricultural sector remains important and will continue to contribute substantially to GNP. At present, it accounts for 23.4 percent of real GDP (against 38.1 percent in 1962). To exploit its climatic advantage, Turkey has in the past decade substantially increased its production of early spring market vegetables in addition to making steady gains in the production of wheat and other traditional products such as hazel nuts, tobacco and dried fruits. Export of these products makes a significant contribution to Turkey's foreign exchange earnings. Cotton, produced in irrigated fields in the Aegean and Adna regions, supplies an expanding textile industry. Although agricultural productivity is rising with the introduction of higher yielding varieties and improved breeds as well as with the increased use of fertilizer and insecticides, Turkish agriculture is still relatively inefficient in comparison with European farming.

Since the 1930s Turkey has been attempting to spur industrialization. The products of its heavy industry facilities, such as steel mills and aluminum plants, are not competitive on the world market. For about two decades, Turkey has also had an assembly industry for automobiles and trucks, electronic goods, and other complex products, the basic parts for which are imported from the west. Light industry has been developing especially rapidly. The textile sector has performed strongly in recent years. Yet on the whole, Turkey still lacks a modernized industrial base which could allow it to meet European competition if present customs protections were removed.

Value added in industry, the growth of which had averaged 10 percent before the crisis, fell by about 2 percent per year during 1978-1980, and by almost 6 percent in 1980, as a result of bottlenecks arising from lack of imported inputs and a proliferation of strikes. With the return to better supply conditions and the end of industrial unrest, this process was reversed in 1981; value added increased by some 7 percent, although from a depressed level. The moderate rate of industrial growth in 1982 (3.2 percent) reflects more accurately the tight monetary policy. Based on 1968 prices, industry's share of the GDP had risen from about 15 percent in 1962 to 23 percent in the 1977-82 period, while the share of agriculture dropped from 38 to 23 percent. A more dramatic rise in the share of industry from 16 to nearly 28 percent, indicated by the figures calculated from current price data, merely reflects the high degree of protection accorded to the industrial sector.

The construction and service sector has grown considerably, attracting many workers who were formerly employed in agriculture. As the sector is heavily dependent on the rate of economic activity as a whole, it has suffered somewhat as the Turkish economy experienced negative growth in recent years. Nonetheless, construction firms have successfully diversified the scope of their operations by obtaining contracts in other Middle Eastern states, where business is much better.

Throughout the period of state planning, the share of the private sector in total investment varied between 42 percent and 52 percent. However, the predominance of state economic enterprises in the developed portion of Turkey's economy has been decreasing in recent years. The inefficiences of state economic enterprises, which are charged with important social welfare roles, impose an intolerable drag on development. As a result, a major concern of the 1980 reform program, agreed upon with the International Monetary Fund, was to put the state economic enterprises on a pay-as-you-go status. That meant huge rises in the prices of their goods and a large reduction in the advantage that these enterprises enjoyed over their private competitors.

Total GDP in 1982 was $52.771 billion. Turkey has had problems in its balance of payments recently, although the situation has been improving. From a $3.4 billion debt in 1977, representing 7 percent of the GNP, the current account deficit has narrowed to a little over $1 billion in 1982 (2 percent of GNP). As a result, inflation has shrunk from a yearly rate of 130 percent in 1980 to current rate of approximately 30 percent.

Foreign remittances in 1982 totaled $2.187 billion; most of this came from Turkish "guest workers" in Western Europe, especially West Germany. The unemployment rate in 1982 was at 12.9 percent.

11. INFRASTRUCTURE. Electricity demand in 1982 was 29,133 KWH, with a shortfall of 2,500 KWH; about 1,773 KWH of electricity was imported from Bulgaria and USSR. There were power shortages in some areas as a result. The development of an extensive road network has been one of the most significant factors for change in Turkey's recent history. In 1983, there were 60,954 km of road. Supplementing the earlier inadequate system of railway lines linking the major urban centers (there are only 10,144 km of railroads), these roads have for the first time brought motor transport to all towns and most villages in Turkey. There were 795,200 passenger cars in Turkey, 397,400 trucks, and 105,800 buses in 1982. This vast increase in communications has contributed to the formation of a national market.

Turkey's major ports are Istanbul, Izmir, Samsun, Mersin, Iskenderun and Trabzon. There is a national airline, Turkish Airlines, which reported 2,421,000 air passengers for 1982. There are two major international airports: Evenboga (30 km from Ankara) and Yesilkoy (28 km from Istanbul).

Improved mobility has worked together with the development of country-wide radio coverage and the availability of television around the major urban centers to end the general isolation of the Turkish village. In 1982, there were 4,404,000 radio sets, 5,084,720 television sets, and 1,501,977 telephones. This has opened even the most remote rural areas to social and economic development as well as to the westernizing influence of ties with Turkish laborers in Europe and elsewhere abroad. The press is very active in Turkey, despite the relatively low literacy rate and relentless government censorship, which has resulted in the closure and suspension of several dailies. While the figures vary, Istanbul is believed to have about 40 dailies, while Ankara has about 25. The five major dailies are Yeni Tanin (Ankara – 300,000), Hurriyet (Istanbul – 750,000 in 1982), Gunaydin (Istanbul – 357,873, suspended Dec. 1982), Tercumen (Istanbul – 515,000, suspended August 1983), Milliyet (Istanbul – 1,050,000, suspended August 1983) and Cumhuriyet (Istanbul – 125,000).

12. SOCIAL SERVICES. The population of Turkey is very young, with about 50 percent under the age of twenty. This adds to the difficulty of providing free education to everyone, as the law requires. Nonetheless, in recent years Turkey has made progress in reducing illiteracy. At present 65 percent of the total population is literate, and a far larger proportion of those of school age can read and write. The illiteracy rate is higher for females and for the rural population. Turkey's educational institutions have burgeoned at all levels in the past decade. The current regime is seeking to slant secondary education more toward technical training to produce graduates better suited to staff the expansion of industry. The number of university students has climbed faster than the economy's ability to absorb graduates in prestigious occupations. Private enterprise, formerly shunned by the most able graduates, is now recruiting a rising proportion of the best students.

Health standards have been steadily improving in Turkey, as evidenced by the declining mortality rate. Nonetheless, Turkey lags behind most European countries in many health indicators. Turkey ranks 66th in the world in per capita medical services. The number of physicians was estimated in 1977 at 56 per 100,000. In that same year, there were 195 hospital beds per 100,000 in the country. Expenditure on health services accounts for 2.5 percent of the budget and 0.6 percent of GNP. Turkey's main problems in this area include the inadequacy of services in many rural regions, and the fact that many Turkish medical graduates (as many as 30 percent in the late seventies) practice in foreign countries, where they can earn a higher income.

Two organizations oversee the social security system in Turkey: the Pension Fund, which covers workers in the public sector, and the Social Insurance Organization, which covers all other workers, except for those engaged in agriculture. Benefits include retirement pensions, disability coverage, marriage grants and death grants.

II. POLITICAL ANALYSIS

1. SUMMARY CONCLUSIONS

1.1 RESOURCES. Turkey's population of 50 million has a rising educational level and increasing skills. Except for hydrocarbons, the state has adequate natural resources to support considerable economic development. It has a climate advantage that favors agricultural sales to Europe as well as to its Middle East neighbors. Turkey is presently self-sufficient in food production with a modest surplus for export. Its combination of geographic location, population size, and economic potential make it among the more significant nations of the world.

1.2 ECONOMY. Turkey has made progress in coping with an extremely severe hyperinflation and foreign exchange crisis which had brought it to the verge of bankruptcy before a comprehensive economic stabilization program was introduced in January 1980. The severity of Turkey's plight forced abandonment of long-held protectionist and autarkic approaches, in favor of opening the economy to market forces along the lines advocated by the International Monetary Fund. The essence of the program involved deep devaluation of Turkish currency, raising public sector prices to realistic levels, stimulating investment, wage restraint, and export promotion. This program, now reinforced by the Ozal government, has cut the wild inflation rate to about one-third of the triple-digit pace that was reached at the end of 1979; it has not yet been possible, however, to meet the government's target of lowering the inflation rate to 25 percent a year. Exports have expanded rapidly, and overseas construction contracts reached some $16 billion, while remittances grew. Thus, considerable improvement has been recorded in Turkey's balance of payments. The stabilization program also made great progress in restoring Turkey's foreign creditworthiness. Ozal's program has yet to score great success in attracting foreign investment, however, or in reducing unemployment. Moreover, his political rivals are critisizing his policies sharply for favoring the wealthy and for risking dissipation of Turkey's hard-won foreign exchange reserves on imported luxury goods.

1.3 POLITICS. Turkey's political scene remains in flux as the country adapts to a new constitutional framework. General Kenan Evren became president with the adoption of the new constitution through a national referendum in 1982. After the legal structure was completed by enactment of an electoral law and a political parties act designed to discourage small parties, national elections were held on November 6, 1983. To improve the chances that one party would secure a parliamentary majority and thus obviate the need for coalition politics, the military rulers had restricted the contest to three organizations which met the stringent requirements for political activity. Despite the last-minute appeal of President Evren to the electorate to vote for the Nationalist Democracy Party, Turgut Ozal's Motherland Party benefited from a modified system of proportional representation to turn the votes of 45 percent of the electorate into control of 53 percent of the seats in the one-house parliament. The Populist Party ran second with just over 30 percent of the vote, and the Nationalist Democracy Party came in last. These parties, which divided all the seats in parliament among themselves, are now confronted by two additional powerful contenders to succeed the left-of-center and right-of-center formations that have dominated Turkey's politics since the Second World War. The municipal elections held on March 25, 1984, over the initial veto of President Evren, confirmed the hold of the Motherland Party on over 43 percent of the electorate, apparently drawn predominantly from the center and right-of-center. But these contests also indicated that the Social Democracy Party of Erdal Inonu commanded the allegiance of most of the left-of-center constituency. The True Path Party, accused of being a continuation of the banned Justice Party, was favored by most of the remaining right-wing voters. Yet, despite their poor showing, the two small parties represented in parliament persisted in their determination to preserve their independent existence, leaving the Turkish political scene badly fragmented.

1.4 THE MILITARY REGIME. Turkey's military rulers duly ceded power to the elected civilian regime. But the constitution accords them considerable latitude, and the influence of the armed forces remains an important political factor. General Evren as President has authority to represent the military as well as limited veto power over legislation and an almost impregnable veto over constitutional amendments for the first six years. The National Security Council was reconstituted as a powerful forum through which civilian rulers must take into serious consideration the views of the ranking officers with respect to broadly defined national security concerns. Finally, the four ranking generals who shared military rule with Evren are acting as advisors to assist him with presidential functions for the next six years. Yet this visible military role, and the general awareness that the armed forces have the potential to step in if political leaders fail, have not deterred the civilian politicians from overriding a presidential veto on the procedures for municipal elections. The president and prime minister are still engaged in a tug of war over the power of appointment to senior offices. And despite the earnest desires of the ranking generals, the civilians have not been discouraged from creating far more political organizations than the framers of the constitution had intended. President Evren has already felt it necessary to warn against efforts to recreate the banned political parties of the previous period of civilian rule.

1.5 PROSPECTS. Turkey's new political structure was designed to prevent the problems of the past. With its specific remedies, it will cope best with future challenges to the extent that they resemble those of the past. The constitutional solutions in the present system are inherently long-term and are not "quick fixes." The shakeout period to determine which parties will last is likely to persist for at least the next four or five years. Major issues will center on Turkey's economic performance, where bureaucratic foot-dragging may hamper somewhat the effort to allow the free play of market forces and the influx of foreign capital. Amnesty and demands to reduce the scope of martial law are certain to be important subjects of debate. The possibility of early elections seems likely to remain controversial, but there is less likelihood of serious party discord over foreign policy. As long as the political debate remains within bounds, the prospect is for increasing military disengagement rather than efforts by the ranking generals to retain maximum involvement in the political process. Attachment to democracy is deeply embedded in Turkish political thinking: military men as well as civilians accept democratic procedure as the only legitimate form of government.

Over the longer run, there are two main sets of dangers that could threaten the extension of civilian rule. First, moves by the banned parties of the previous era to resume operation or progress by the extreme left or right to regain political legitimacy would be profoundly destablizing. Second, recrudescence of politically-motivated terrorism in conjunction with ideological agitation would pose an immediate provocation to the Turkish armed forces. Turkey's rulers are aware of these menaces and are on their guard to fend them off.

2. POLITICAL STRUCTURE

2.1 POLITICAL INSTITUTIONS. Turkey's most recent period of military rule bequeathed the state a new system of political institutions. Cornerstone of the structure is a constitution ratified by 91 percent of those who voted in a nation-wide referendum in November 1982. The constitution is designed to prevent a repetition of the difficulties that preceded the military intervention in 1980. Thus, it balances a perceived need for governmental authority with respect for the fundamental rights and freedoms mandated in the European Convention on Human Rights. It details the social and economic rights of citizens, while committing the state to provide a wide spectrum of social services. Yet it makes clear in greater detail than in most European constitutions the circumstances under which individual rights and freedoms can be curtailed. For the first six years, it gives the president such enhanced veto power over constitutional amendments that changes to which he objects are all but ruled out.

New Structure. Turkey's system of checks and balances has been redirected in the interests of assuring stronger government, but with a concern not to permit a majority party to run roughshod over the rights of the opposition. Heart of the new structure is a one-house parliament of 400 members elected for five-year terms; this single-chamber assembly replaced the more unwieldly two-house structure with half again as many members in total, which had failed to act decisively during the previous period of civilian rule. Every Turkish citizen over age 30, except for members of the judiciary, professors, civil servants, and members of the military, is eligible to serve as a deputy, providing he has completed primary education, has met the military service obligation, and has not been convicted of major crimes (pardons for offenses related to treason, terrorism, and anarchy would not remove this disqualification).

A primary concern of the framers of the new parliamentary system was to obviate the need for a coalition government to the greatest extent possible. This aim was to be achieved by two basic mechanisms: assuring that the party receiving a plurality of votes would be overrepresented in the assembly, and discouraging the creation and survival of parties representing only a small fraction of the electorate. Indications during the lengthy effort to draft the new constitution made clear that the military rulers would have liked to assure a two-party structure, but they evidently could not divine how to do so directly without running against their faith in the wisdom of the people at large. Their problem was compounded by their apparent suspicion of politicans, a mistrust that led the military leaders to hedge the new system with numerous provisions to prevent a narrow national oligarchy from perpetually dominating political parties.

Proportional Representation. Overrepresentaiton of the largest party in parliament was assured by the electoral system of modified proportional representation, the so-called D'Hont system. Candidates are to run in province-wide constituencies or from electoral districts fashioned from groups of counties in the larger provinces. The election law specifies that parties whose nationwide vote in general elections does not exceed a barrier of 10 percent of the valid ballots cast will be ineligible to receive seats in the assembly. In multi-member electoral districts (the almost invariable case), a party must receive votes in excess of the number of valid ballots cast divided by the number of seats to be allocated in order to qualify for deputyships in that constituency. In effect, the modified proportional system distributed these unawarded deputyships disproportionately among those parties qualifying for seats. In order to accentuate the chances for one party to win a majority, voting is by party list only, or for one independent candidate, no matter how many seats are in question Provisions to discourage the multiplication of parties revolved around requiring a prospective political party to meet substantial size conditions. Thus, in order to go into operation, a party had to have at least 30 founding members. Moreover, for a party to take part in elections, it had to have completed its organization in at least 34 of the 67 provinces. Further, if a party failed to compete in two successive general elections, it would be closed by court order.

2.2 THE EXECUTIVE. The constitution divides executive power between the president, the prime minister, and other independent agencies, such as the National Security Council and the Higher Education Council. Basically a parliamentary structure, the Turkish system accords the prime minister and his cabinet the lion's share of responsiblity for the supervision and implementation of government policy. The prime minister selects the other ministers, who are confirmed and serve at the pleasure of the parliament. Cabinet ministers are jointly responsible with the prime minister for carrying out government policy. The cabinet is free to take what decisions it pleases, but its acts may be referred to the Constitutional Court for a ruling on constitutionality.

The president is to be elected by parliament to a single seven-year term. But as a special case for the first incumbent under the 1982 constitution, adopted by popular referendum, General Evren was inaugurated to the presidency in November 1982. In subsequent presidential elections, the votes of a two-thirds majority of parliament will be needed for election on the first or second ballot, or a simple majority if a third vote is requried. A fourth round runoff between the top two contenders would follow if need be. Should a fourth ballot fail to decide the contest, new parliamentary elections would take place.

As head of state, the president enjoys great symbolic authority. In addition, he has the specific mandate to assure the smooth operation of state organs through the convening of parliament when necessary, returning laws (except for the budget) to the legislature for reconsideration, submitting constitutional amendments to popular referendum if he deems fit, referring to the constitutional court laws he believes may be unconstitutional, and exercising the power of amnesty or sentence reduction for convicts. He appoints the prime minister and selects other major officials in the executive and judiciary. Among his important functions is to serve as commander-in-chief of the Turkish armed forces as well as to convene and preside over the National Security Council; those duties suggest that the presidency will be reserved for former ranking officers and is unlikely ever to be held by a pure civilian. Nevertheless, except for his powers of appointment and amnesty, the president, for the most part, shares responsibility with the cabinet, the parliament, or the judiciary, unless specified extraordinary circumstances of parliamentary paralysis obtain. Indeed, the president alone has little authority to block a government once it has been seated.

2.3 THE JUDICIARY. An independent judiciary has long existed in Turkey; its status is confirmed in the provisions of the 1982 constitution. This structure includes a Constitutional Court of eleven regular and four substitute members, selected by the president from three nominees for each seat proposed by the other senior judicial bodies, the Higher Education Council, and senior administrative officers and lawyers. Justices serve on good behavior until age 65. In addition to ruling on the constitutionality of laws, the court is charged with deciding cases involving the closure of political parties. The court has the right of item veto in ruling on laws or decrees, and is not obligated to invalidate a whole act in order to overturn a single provision. Finally, the court has the authority to try the president, the prime minister, and other senior officials for offenses relating to their functions. In the Turkish system, other superior courts for penal, administrative, and military affairs have final jurisdiction over matters in their purview; the decisions of these civilian and military tribunals are not reviewed by the Constitutional Court.

2.4 POLITICAL PARTIES. Political parties are integral to the new structure, although the spectrum for political organization is limited in comparision with the broader limits permitted before 1980. Leftist parties and organizations of the extreme right are banned, as are groups that seek to trade on religion. To encourage national unity and discourage divisiveness, all parties are obliged to accept Ataturkism, the shorthand formula for Ataturk's program of secular westernization. Further, to diminish the heat of political partisanship, parties are prohibited from establishing women's branches, nor are they permitted to set up affiliates in villages or sub-districts. (Yet, at the same time, perhaps to impart a more conservative cast to the operation of the political system, rural areas were accorded greater weight in the structure than in the past by increasing the number of representatives for smaller provinces while the total number of deputies in parliament was reduced.) With an eye to prevent the politicization of the universities, parties are forbidden to organize youth branches. University students are ineligible to become members of political parties. Moreover, the age to be able to join a party was raised from 18 to 21.

Unbridled partisanship is discouraged by new regulations regarding the switching of political party allegiance by parliamentary deputies. Competition to lure deputies to overturn parliamentary majorities by changing parties had been the bane of the preceding parliamentary period. Thus the 1982 constitution provided that deputies who leave the party on whose ticket they were elected can remain in parliament as independents, but they cannot join another party during that legislative term without loss of their seats unless a majority in parliament rules otherwise. A deputy elected on one party's slate cannot be put on the ticket of another party in the immediately succeeding election without winning a primary.

A number of new legal provisions limit the dominance of the national headquarters of parties over their provincial organizations. The right of party leaders to disregard local preferences in nominating candidates for national office is restricted. With the exception of the 1983 contests, primary elections by the party membership in each electoral district are required. To weaken the national leadership's control still further, the political parties law calls for party chairmen to serve no more than twelve years without a four-year break in office. Provincial chairmen as well must be changed every ten years at the maximum. The new system provides that party chairmen are to be elected by secret ballot of the national convention. Moreover, the law prohibits binding decisions from being imposed on parliamentary caucus members by fiat of the national leadership. Such decisions can be taken only by secret ballot of the caucus.

The new structure is designed to limit the influence of special interests on the party system. Parties are prohibited from links to international organizations. Pressure groups, especially labor unions, are not permitted to affiliate with or provide support to political parties. Moreover, donations to parties are limited in amount to 1 million Turkish lira (about $2,800 at mid-1984 exchange rates) per year; in any event, deputies may not contribute more than their salary to their political organizations. Parties may not receive loans from or extend credit to any persons or institutions.

Despite these limitations, parties enjoy a commanding advantage over independents. Only those individuals who through tribal or other mechanisms can mobilize large blocs of supporters have any chance to challenge party dominance. Few Turkish voters were willing to waste their votes in 1983 by selecting one independent in a multimember constituency, thereby losing the opportunity to vote for the rest of the slate. It is no accident, therefore, that in these contests not one single individual who ran as an independent and not on a party ticket was elected to office.

2.5 POLITICAL LEADERSHIP. The adjustment to civilian rule is still continuing in Turkish political life. President Kenan Evren, the senior general who led the military intervention in 1980, remains a powerful political personality. A fatherly figure, whose no-nonsense approach won him many followers, Evren serves as the voice of the military establishment, an institution that sees itself and is seen as the ultimate guardian of the new democratic order. Although his powers are not nearly as extensive as they were under the period of military rule, he still commands wide respect and moral authority. The civilian leaders are careful to coordinate their activities with him. Politicians take his pronouncements seriously, even if they are willing to defy his positions on such important political issues as the law speeding up the timetable for the 1984 municipal elections.

The principal leaders of the political parties of the second republican constitutional period (1961-1980) are ruled out of political life for ten years according to Temporary Article 4 of the 1982 constitution. A new crop of political figures has taken their place. Chief among these is Turgut Ozal, the prime minister, who came to power at the head of the Motherland Party (Anavatan Partisi). Former economic czar in the last Demirel cabinet who continued for the first two years of military rule, Ozal has made his mark as an appealing and able politician. His track record in the economic realm and his political experience gave him a decided advantage in the three-way race permitted in the 1983 elections. He clearly attracted a majority of the centrist and right-of-center vote. His personal piety may have won him the support of the more religiously observant constituency as well. Decisive and bold, he wasted no time in December 1983 in implementing the most far-reaching liberal economic experiment that Turkey has ever experienced. And his prestige rose further after his party's strong showing in the municipal elections in March 1984, which were widely regarded as a referendum on the performance of the government.

The leader of the Nationalist Democracy Party (NDP), ex-general Turgut Sunlap, was popularly identified with the military regime. His party's poor showing in the 1983 elections indicates that he has little hold on the traditional right-of-center constituency. His party has lost adherents to the emerging True Path Party (Dogru Yol

Partisi), an organization in which former Justice Party politicans appear to be playing a major part. Although Sunlap's leadership was sharply questioned after his party ran last of all the major contenders in the municipal elections in 1984, he was thereafter reelected chairman of the NDP. He has vowed to continue political competition, despite persistent erosion of his party's following.

Yildirim Avci, head of the True Path Party, was catapulted into national prominence when he was selected to leave his position as a provincial functionary in the Ministry of Health to participate in the Constituent Assembly in 1981. His brother had been a Justice Party deputy from Denizli province, and the family apparently had good connections with former Justice Party leader Suleyman Demirel. Avci's campaign speeches gave broad hints that the True Path Party was the continuation of the Democrat Party of the first republican constitutional pariod as well as the successor to the Justice Party. Embittered by the ban on his party's running in the 1983 general elections, Avci waged an often personally abusive campaign against Turgut Ozal in the municipal elections, where he sought the allegiance of the right-of-center constituency. It was apparently his relationship with the leadership of the defunct Justice Party which accounted for the relatively good performance of his party in the 1984 contests rather than his own personal appeal. Legal moves to close his party for being too closely linked to the banned Justice Party call into question his political future.

The leadership of the left-of-center constituency is also in flux. Necdet Calp, leader of the Populist Party, ran more strongly than was generally expected in the 1983 contests. An administrator, who served as provincial governor as well as private secretary to Prime Minister Inonu, he had also filled the post of Undersecretary in the Prime Ministry for the first two years of the military regime. Calp was not able to retain the allegiance of the left-of-center voters when the municipal elections allowed wider political competition, and his party ran well behind the Social Democracy Party (SODEP) under Erdal Inonu, son of Turkey's most revered leader after Ataturk. Although Calp kept his campaign pledge to resign as party president if his organization got less votes than SODEP, he was reelected to his party post.

Erdal Inonu, a physics professor who had served as dean and rector of the Middle East Technical University, had not sought a political career until 1983. But his obvious advantage in voter recognition as the embodiment of the banned Republican Party, which had been led for many years by his father, gave him a clear head start in the quest for left-of-center votes. His considerable aura of legitimacy was not sufficient to assure that his party could compete in the 1983 general elections, but he was able to qualify to compete in the municipal contests the following year. Although he was not able to turn his prestige into victories in Turkey's largest cities, which had in the past elected Republican Peoples Party mayors, the nearly 25 percent of the whole vote which his party polled nation-wide confirmed him as a political force to be reckoned with on the Turkish scene.

2.6 ROLE OF THE MILITARY. Pride and respect for the military runs deep in Turkey. Its 550,000-man force is a functioning part of the NATO defense establishment. Although Turkey's military equipment does not meet NATO standards and economic difficulties put the country in the status of an aid recipient from its allies, its men are well-trained and highly disciplined soldiers. The Turkish armed forces are on their own fully capable of carrying out their mission to defend the country against all Turkey's smaller neighbors.

Having intervened in politics three times in recent decades (1960, 1971, and 1980), the officer corps clearly plays an important political role. The military establishment regards itself as the guardian of national security, a role acknowledged in the constitution. Since the early 1960s, political activity in the armed forces has been kept subject to the chain of command; it is the generals who decide how to express the political will of the whole establishment. The National Security Council, created after the 1960 intervention and reformed under new membership after the military ceded power in November 1983, provides the forum for senior generals to raise political issues with their civilian counterparts. Indeed, the 1982 constitution (Art. 118) mandates that the cabinet must "take into urgent consideration" decisions of the National Security Council on matters of internal and external security. Martial law continues under the civilian regime, as the Turkish leadership accepts the proposition that danger from terrorists and ethnic separatists is not past. But the military establishment clearly agrees that forceful, direct military intervention into the political arena reflects exceptional circumstances. The members of the armed forces acknowledge their subordination to elected civilians, and the senior generals display concern not to allow the military establishment to become politicized by continuing involvement in politics.

2.7 RELIGION. Multiparty competition has made religion the object of political exploitation. Ataturk's efforts to separate religion and state as well as to deemphasize Muslim practice did not break the hold of Islamic traditions in the villages. He was more successful in weaning the intelligentsia away from attachment to Islam. Particularly in the past 15 years, small parties have been tempted to seek votes from the traditionally-oriented masses by capitalizing on religious interests. Regarding the National Salvation Party's appeal to the religious vote as dangerous to national unity and to the sovereignty of the secular state, the Turkish leadership has made certain that prohibition against this behavior is reinforced in the law, and constitution. Fundamental regulations call for the state to supervise religious education. Nonetheless, it is difficult to prevent subtle play on religious feeling, and it is unlikely that religious considerations can be entirely extirpated from the Turkish political scene. In fact, Prime Minister Ozal's religious background appears to have been a factor in attracting the votes to his Motherland Party.

The importance of religion in Turkey, however, has gone beyond its role in interparty competition. Clashes between Sunnis and Alevis, culminating in the sectarian conflict at Kahramanmaras in December 1978 which saw over 100 killed in two days of intercommunal fighting, have left scars which will take time to heal. It is not clear how these communal differences will manifest themselves under the civilian regime.

The Khomeini revolution in neighboring Iran has had little impact on the state of religious controversy in Turkey. With their strong secular bent, the Alevis in Turkey were not attracted by the religious teachings of their fellow Shiites in Iran. Conservative Turkish Sunnis have for some years been successful in encouraging greater religious observance. Thus, such practices as a return to the headscarf for women appear to be gaining ground, and greater attention is paid to religious celebrations such as Ramadan. To propitiate Islamic feelings, the Minister of Education in May 1984 decreed more modest dress for girls in the annual gymnastic performance memorializing Ataturk's start of the struggle for independence. Although such government concessions to religious sensitivities alarm Ataturkist secularists, there seems little likelihood that the increasing attention to Islamic practice seriously threatens the laic basis of the Turkish regime. Commitment to Turkey as a secular state is explicitly enshrined in the 1983 constitution as it had been in previous constitutions.

2.8 FACTORS FOR STABILITY. Turkey's resilience has been demonstrated by its smooth return to multiparty politics on the timetable set by the military. This accomplishment reflects the widely-shared commitment to parliamentary government and to the competition of parties. The broad national consensus on the general directions set by Ataturk for Turkey provides a framework within which those of many differing political philosophies can cooperate. The need for rapid development is universally accepted, although subsidiary questions of how much liberalization Turkey can take are still matters of partisan contention. Turkey's western vocation is opposed by only a tiny minority, although the matter of when and how to seek full membership in the European Communities remains a disputed issue. A deep sense of patriotism and loyalty to the state has played a major role in enabling the populace to adapt to interruptions in the normal political practice.

Turkish society has important strengths as well. As adept organizers, the Turks have created a variegated civil society with a rich panoply of institutions, including an array of political, labor, business, professional, cultural, and social organizations. While some of the more extremist organizations in various fields have been banned, this ramified structure forms a strong base for the return to democratic political practice. In addition, the rising educational level of the Turkish population gives greater opportunity for adapting to new conditions than in the past. The inventory of skills is expanding. And there is a depth of leadership that suggests that Turkey will be able to overcome the difficult problems that confront it.

2.9 CHALLENGES. Turkey will need these strengths to deal with its challenges. The stresses and strains of a developing society have confounded governments in the past. The flow of population off the farms and into the cities threatens the traditional patterns of politics. These changes have contributed to eroding constraints on political extremism. Terrorism became the paramount challenge to the system as migrants to the cities brought their age-old methods of settling scores into the crowded squatter settlements, and as leftist and rightist student radicals branched out from intramural contests to attack the state. Organized in a number of conspiratorial groups, the perpetrators of political violence have proven difficult to eradicate or deter completely. Despite the relative success of martial law under the military rulers, such conspiratorial groups continue to operate, although they no longer appear to present a major challenge to the state.

An enduring question for Turkey is the tension between partisan advantage and the national interest. Politicians in the past have fastened on issues in ways that advanced their own party fortunes rather than contributing to consensus and cooperation with their political rivals. Continuation of this pattern in the constitutional period is already visible in the partisan rhetoric of the competing parties. There is also an underlying current of discontent fed by the former politicial leaders who are ruled out of competition for power. It remains to be seen whether the new crop of political leaders will be more adept than their predecessors at keeping the fine balance between partisanship and the need to concert for the public good.

Finally, equitable economic development remains an open question in Turkey. The economic vulnerability of Turkish society has grown as the rural community has been brought increasingly into the money economy and the national market. Rising unemployment became more visible and has more serious consequences as a result of migration to the cities. At the same time, the unbalance in regional development and underdeveloped state of the Anatolian hinterland became more apparent. Thus, the impact and scope of inflation were far more severe in the 1970s than they had been in the 1960s. Economic insecurity continues to be one of the major issues confronting the Turkish population at large. While the turn toward becoming an export-oriented economy has improved the balance of payments, the domestic industrial sector continues to suffer from stagnant demand and underutilization of capacity. Much of the current political contest will turn on the success of the liberalization program and on who benefits and to what extent from the new measures.

3.
RECENT DEVELOPMENTS: 1975-1983

3.1 INTERNAL DEVELOPMENTS - POLITICAL. The inability of the civilians to deal effectively with Turkey's descent into political chaos in the latter half of the 1970s led the generals on the National Security Council to take over the government on September 12, 1980. Political violence growing out of a contest between small groups of leftist and rightist extremists had spread beyond the campuses and labor precincts to which it had earlier been confined. These groups directed their attacks primarily against each other, although unintended victims died as the conflict moved into the streets. Eventually, the security forces became a target for assassionation by leftist extremists of the Revolutionary Path and Revolutionary Left organizations which were successors to the notorious Turkish Peoples Liberation Army of the late 1960s. These revolutionaries, many trained by the Palestinians and inspired by the doctrines of Soviet Communism as well as later Trotskyist, Maoist, and Third World variants, hoped to bring down the reigme, although they did not generally target major political figures. Before being stopped by the military's intervention, this mounting violence was claiming more than 20 victims a day and appeared impervious to the measures taken by the civilian authorities.

The challenge to national unity from Kurdish separatism in eastern Turkey added to the grave concern in the military establishment. Agitation of tiny Kurdish groups was supported by the left-wing Turkish Labor Party. This organization's calls for greater Kurdish cultural autonomy led the Ankara government to suspend it after the military intervention in 1971. But both agitation by Kurdish dissidents and leftist support for Kurdish causes resumed in the mid-1970s, despite the imposition of martial law in the eastern provinces where most Kurds resided. While some of the disorder in the Kurdish areas represented lawless elements rather than a serious effort at separatism, Ankara's military leaders interpreted the dissidence as a major threat to national unity.

The senior officers were also highly concerned over the growing tendency to exploit religion for political purposes. The premier example was the manipulation of religious symbolism by the National Salvation Party. Its trafficking in religion culminated in an assembly in Konya on September 6, 1980, when, before national television, party members dressed in religious colors sat down during the Turkish national anthem. While the vote of the National Salvation Party had declined over the decade of the 1970s from a high of 12 percent to only 8 percent, the mounting stridency of its propaganda put an increasingly disruptive cast on its activities.

These deleterious trends took place against a backdrop of general political paralysis created by the bickering of parties unused to the need for the give and take of coalition politics. In the 1970s, neither the right-of-center Justice Party nor the left-of-center Republican Peoples' Party was able to win a majority in parliament. As a result, lengthy interregnums under caretaker cabinets punctuated the political contest, testifying to the unwillingness of party leaders to compromise. Right-of-center and left-of-center coalitions succeeded each other every few years. In these circumstances, the fear of the major coalition partner of alienating essential minor party support destroyed any possibility for decisive action. Indeed, the parliament all but ceased to function after March 1980, when the Turkish body politic was treated to the spectacle of six months of futile parliamentary balloting in the effort to elect a president after Fahri Koruturk's term ended. Over 120 rounds of balloting had still failed to fill that office at the time when the military moved to take over in September 1980.

Partisan efforts to apply a spoils system to the bureaucracy crippled the administration just at the time when the parliamentary deadlock was frustrating policy leadership. Starting with well-publicized efforts to replace career officials with party loyalists in the radio and television administration, these partisan wrangles spread to such other ministries as customs, interior, and justice. The impartiality of government mechanisms fell into serious question. As a result, even martial law, imposed in 1977 after secratian violence in Kahramanmaras, was unable to slow the rate of killings.

3.2 MILITARY REGIME. The generals under Kenan Evren took power only after the civilians disregarded a series of warnings to pull together in the interests of effective government. While the military leaders disbanded parliament immediately, they soon announced that they would convene a constituent assembly to prepare a new constitution, electoral law, and political parties law. Thus, the generals made clear from the start their intention to return to civilian political practice. Their model appeared to be a compromise between the all-powerful parliament of the Ataturk period and the extensive checks and balances of the second constitutional period (1961-1980). However, the generals celebrated their move as a return to "Ataturkism," implying that to remedy deviations from Ataturk's secularist nationalism was their principal goal. They regarded the challenges facing Turkey's body politic as more serious than those which triggered previous military interventions, thereby justifying the need for a several-year transition and extensive alternations in the system.

The government of technocrats installed by the generals on September 16, 1980, worked effectively with the military authorities to restore law and order. Suspension of normal constitutional immunities permitted the regime to sweep up a broad range of suspects and hold them, originally for 90 days, then 45 days, before bringing charges. This activist policy rapidly curtailed expression of opinion by closing all organs of the extreme left and right as well as preventing all serious criticism of the military regime.

The populace welcomed the respite from terrorism, which had made many citizens reluctant to venture out. Parents, especially, were relieved that educational institutions were no longer the scene of violent battles between right and left. There seems little question that the majority of Turks saw the generals as genuine protectors of the state, rather than as grasping for power for selfish reasons.

Not surprisingly the seriousness of the generals about ceding power in due course did not satisfy the former civilian leaders. The major party heads were freed after an initial short period of incarceration in Canakkale, immediately following the military takeover. As part of the bargain, they signed pledges to refrain from political activity and from making public statements. But they refused to endorse the generals' moves toward establishing a new constitutional system. It was the lack of enthusiasm of the former party chiefs for the procedure to select members of the constituent assembly that led the generals in October 1981 to announce that all previous political parties were dissolved. Bulent Ecevit, who had resigned as head of the Republican Peoples Party shortly after the 1980 military takeover, was jailed for a short time. Necmettin Erbakan of the religiously-oriented National Salvation Party and Alparslan Turkes of the proto-fascist Nationalist Movement Party were also imprisoned for acts committed prior to 1980. Erbakan was subsequently released, but Turkes remained incarcerated. Suleyman Demirel was sent to a second period of enforced residence in Canakkale in the summer of 1983 for involvement in the Great Turkey Party, an organization closed by the military rulers as a direct attempt to recreate the banned Justice Party of which he had been leader. In reaction, the generals added temporary provisions to the constitution excluding all previous civilian party leaders from political life for ten years. Those who had been senators or deputies in the last civilian parliament prior to 1980 were forbidden to hold office in the new parties for five years.

3.3 TOWARD CIVILIAN RULE. The military rulers kept to their announced timetable to return to elections. They restricted the field to three parties by vetoing founders of all other parties, thereby preventing these organizations from qualifying to take part in the electoral contests. While this action left these parties in existence but unable to campaign for the 1983 general elections, the military rulers went further in formally abolishing the Great Turkey Party. On the other hand, they took steps to favor the Nationalist Democracy Party, which made available a spot on its ticket for the prime minister of the military period, Bulend Ulsu, to run as an independent. In an effort to boost the chances of this party, President Evren made a special appeal on the eve of the elections to solicit votes for this organization. Nonetheless, the military permitted Turgut Ozal, at the head of a private enterprise party, and Necdet Calp, as leader of a social-democratic style party, to complete the requirements necessary to compete in the elections. The military rulers carefully vetted the candidates put up by all three of the parties eligible for the 1983 elections, vetoing about one-fifth of the candidates from each of the three organizations. The generals also vetoed the candidacies of some 90 percent of the host of independent aspirants who had sought to enter these contests. The aim in so doing was obviously to assure uncluttered lists in order to facilitate a decisive victory by one party in the elections.

3.4 REORGANIZATION. On other fronts, the military sought to curb some of the institutions which the generals believed had been responsible for encouraging terrorism. In the education field, considered the prime incubator of terrorists, the military rulers on November 6, 1981, set up a Higher Education Council (YOC) to provide tight central direction to what had been a partially decentralized system of individual universities. The Higher Education council, headed by the powerful educational administrator, Ihsan Dogramaci, and composed of 25 members, mostly appointed by President Evren or by the Minister of Education, was given extensive responsibilities. According to the law reorganizing the educational system, university governing bodies would henceforth be appointed, not elected by the professors as in the past. The Council could transfer teachers to unpopular universities; those refusing to go would be penalized in promotions. The Council also received authority to suspend those professors who were judged not to be performing properly or who opposed Council directives. Finally, in a far-reaching move to end the thorny problem of perennial student status for those who merely gained admittance to the universities, the new law provided that students had only six years to finish a four-year curriculum or seven years to complete a five-year program. Using its extensive powers, the Council dismissed some 50 professors and refused to renew the contracts of several hundred others. In order to avoid the possiblity of similar action against them, hundreds of other professors resigned or retired, thus preserving the possibility of returning to the universities after the advent of civilian government.

Labor was another area reorganized by the generals. The left-leaning Confederation of Revolutionary Labor Unions (DISK) was considered by the generals to be responsible for the wave of politically-motivated strikes which had hurt the economy and dissuaded foreign investment in the period before the 1980 military intervention. The martial law regime immediately closed the Confederation, which represented about a quarter of organized labor in Turkey, charging that DISK engaged in "mass terrorist activities" to promote the dominance of the working class. The authorities charged that one of the main unions in the Confederation published terrorist and secessionist propaganda. DISK was accused of echoing the positions of the World Federation of Trade Unions based in Prague. Small rightist and religiously oriented confederations of unions were also closed down. Turkey's largest union confederation, Turk-Is, with more than one million members, was permitted to continue operating. A moderate pro-government organization, Turk-Is was not blamed for the labor ills of the pre-military intervention period. Under military rule this confederation displayed an independent position in pushing for a higher minimum wage than the generals wished. It was so important for the regime to leave this large labor body operating that it enjoyed a measure of immunity. Turk-Is used this immunity to resist changes in labor laws proposed by the military establishment.

Another sector which faced far stricter regulation as a result of the military intervention was the press. The generals enforced a rigorous ban on political propaganda, taking away at one stroke much of the normal grist of the newspaper world. To back up this prohibition, left-wing papers were summarily closed. Cumhuriyet, a left-leaning establishment organ, was shut several time for violating millitary restrictions. Other papers were also suspended from time to time for criticism, even implied, of the military regime; the ban on public questioning of acts of the period of military rule has continued ever since. A new press law was passed, increasing the educational requirements to publish newspapers or practice journalism. The press became extremely bland in comparison with its previous feistiness. And while this blandness was attenuated once political activity resumed in preparation for the 1983 elections, the scope of press opinion remained limited even after the return to civilian rule, and commentators were careful not to write inflammatory material.

3.5 ECONOMIC. The military regime took over unchanged the economic stabilization program initiated by the last civilian government in January 1980. That plan involved a determined effort to reduce government spending by putting state economic enterprises on a pay-as-you-go basis. It called for deep and continuous adjustments of the value of the Turkish lira to keep the domestic price structure in line with that of the world market. The program emphasized export promotion as the only lasting remedy for Turkey's chronic balance of payments problem. It freed interest rates to make lending money attractive. And it set out to attract foreign capital by extending new guarantees and a more favorable climate.

Whereas this program was put into effect by government decree under the old regime, thus bypassing the need for parliamentary approval, one aspect which could not be accomplished in this way was improved income distribution. The revision of the tax laws was not possible until the generals took over, ending the parliamentary paralysis that prevented the enactment of almost all legislation.

The effects of this total reform program were not long in appearing. The International Monetary Fund and the international lending community accepted Turkey's performance as meeting the requirements of sound development. International assistance in the amount of some $1.16 billion for 1981 was immediately forthcoming. The financial boost was sufficient to relieve Turkey's short-term foreign exchange pinch. Imports steadied at $8.5 billion in 1982 as a result of sharply higher price tags, while exports began to rise, reaching $5.69 billion in 1982. Worker remittances also spurted to $2.35 billion in 1982 in response to the more realistic exchange rates. After an initial fillip as wages were adjusted, inflation steadily slowed. By the end of 1982, the inflation rate had fallen to about a third of that of 1980. Domestic production, which had actually decreased in 1979 and 1980, began slowly edging upward in 1981; in 1982, GDP increased just over four percent. It rose another four percent the following year.

3.6 EXTERNAL DEVELOPMENTS – ARAB STATES. Until recent decades, Republican Turkey had refrained from involvement in the Arab world; its modern political and economic interests were with the West and it had no desire to rekindle memories of the Ottoman past. The Baghdad Pact (later CENTO), a grandiose effort to galvanize the Middle East under Turkey's leadership, seems to have been an aberration. Starting in 1964, however, successive Turkish regimes began avidly to court Arab support in the United Nations in connection with the Cyprus crisis. After the United States first embargoed military aid to Turkey in 1975, simultaneously cutting off Turkish access to all American-controlled weaponry, the Turks turned even more urgently to the Arab Middle East for assistance. The shutoff of the flow of Turkish workers to Europe after 1973 added impetus to efforts to develop markets and trading partners in the Arab world. The rapid rise in petroleum prices after the oil crisis of 1973 also made the search for an assured energy supply at reasonable prices increasingly urgent.

While Turkish ties with the Arab world have thus intensified for both political and economic reasons, this improvement has not been shared equally by all. Syria, for example, remains essentially estranged because of the loss of the Hatay (or Alexandretta) to Turkey in 1938.

Moreover, Turkey has been concerned by the degree of Soviet influence in Damascus and by the extent of Syrian involvement with Turkish terrorists. Iraq and Libya, in contrast, have especially close relations with Ankara: they supply oil and are large markets for Turkish business abroad. Saudi Arabia has not been as responsive to Turkish overtures as many Turkish leaders had hoped, although private Turkish firms have established growing economic relationships, especially important for construction and the export of Turkish labor. Saudi Arabia and Turkey have collaborated in diplomatic efforts within the context of the Islamic movement. Turkish sympathy for Egypt has grown since the death of Nasser, who condemned Turkey's western ties. But Egypt's relative isolation within the Arab world since Camp David made the Turks reluctant to give emphasis to improved Turco-Egyptian relations.

3.7 ISLAMIC STATES. Turkey's quest for international support led it to look beyond its Arab neighbors. Turkey joined the Islamic Conference in 1976 and hosted its meeting in Istanbul that same year. The Turks have sought ever since to use this forum to mobilize support for their position on Cyprus. Thus, it became particularly urgent for President Evren to be the first Turkish chief of state to participate in a meeeting of the Islamic summit in Casablanca in January 1984, following on the heels of the Unilateral Declaration of Independence of Northern Cyprus a few months before.

Relations with non-Arab Islamic states have improved considerably improved in recent times. After a stressful start in the early years of the Khomeini regime, when Tehran appeared concerned that Iranian exiles might use Turkish territory to support a restoration of the monarchy, relations between the two states expanded. Iran is now Turkey's largest trading partner, supplying a significant portion of Turkey's oil at favorable prices as well as purchasing food and manufactured goods from the Turks. Initiatives to restore the Regional Cooperation for Development, which had linked the two with Pakistan in earlier years, are underway. President Zia ul-Haq of Pakistan was the first chief of state to visit Turkey after the September 1980 military takeover. Turkey and Pakistan are participating in the Islamic Good Will delegation to mediate the Iraq-Iran war. Bangladesh and Indonesia also have close ties with Turkey.

3.8 ISRAEL. During the years when Turkey paid little attention to the Arab world, it established diplomatic relations with Israel. After 1956, Turkey recalled its ambassador and was represented for many years by a senior charge; Israel was permitted only similar representation in Ankara. As its relationships with the Arabs intensified in the late 1970s, Turkey came under pressure to break diplomatic relations with Israel altogether. In the wake of the 1980 vote by the Israeli Knesset to enact the Guela Cohen bill annexing Jerusalem, the Turkish government announced it would reduce its diplomatic representation to the second secretary level. Turkey opposed Israel's military intervention in Lebanon in 1982 and called on all foreign forces to leave that country. Ankara has subsequently spoken out on a number of occasions to criticize "the intransigent and expansionist policy of Israel" which "hinders peace." Nonetheless, economic and cultural ties between the two countries have not been greatly affected by the worsening political relationship. Moreover, Turkey is not likely to reduce further its diplomatic relations with Israel. To do so could damage Turkey's key associations with allies such as the United States.

3.9 THE PLO. Along with the swing toward the Arabs, Turkey has given increasing recognition and status to the PLO. Faruk Kaddumi met with the Turkish Foreign Minister in 1976. Despite the involvement of the "Eagles of the Palestinian Revolution Organization" in an attack on the Egyptian embassy in Ankara in July 1979, in which two Turkish guards were killed, the relationship continues to grow closer. PLO leaders, who mediated the surrender of the Palestinian gunmen in the Egyptian embassy at that time, won reconfirmation of their right to open an office in Ankara with diplomatic status. This PLO office has operated since October 1979, when Arafat inaugurated its activities while on an official visit at the invitation of the Turkish Prime Minister. Turkey has repeatedly indicated that it favors the restoration of rights to the Palestinian people, including the right to establish a state.

3.10 THE WEST – THE U.S. Turkey's main foreign tie is with the United States. Since the end of the Second World War, Ankara has looked to Washington for military and economic assistance. The Turks have received over $8 billion in aid during this period. The United States embargo on military aid, imposed in 1975 in response to the Turkish intervention in Cyprus, was a painful foreign policy experience for Turkey. Although popular frustration against the United States was bitterly vented at this time, cooler heads prevailed in negotiating the official relationship. Turkey moved slowly in retaliating; it acted to suspend American access to bilateral facilities only after the U.S. Congress reconfirmed the embargo in a second vote in July 1975. These facilities remained closed even after aid was partially restored a few months later, until the U.S. Congress in 1978 completely lifted all restrictions on military supplies to Turkey and negotiations opened for a new Defense and Economic Cooperation Agreement. The signing of this accord in 1980 put mutual relations back on course. Turkish-American relations have improved steadily ever since. United States participation in international economic assistance efforts to rescue the Turkish economy from collapse in 1980 were recognized as a key to this effort. United States responsiveness contrasted favorably in Turkish eyes with the less enthusiastic support of Europeans, whose willingness to contribute was dampened by the military takeover in September 1980. The American media's sympathetic interpretation of the circumstances that brought the military to power in Turkey also helped erase lingering ill-feeling over the embargo years.

3.11 WESTERN EUROPE. The NATO alliance with European states has been the cornerstone of Turkey's foreign policy in the period since the Second World War. These relations have grown deeper and more intimate as the revival of European economies provided greater markets and aid for Turkey. The exception has been Greece, with which relations deteriorated during this period because of the opposing positions of Athens and Ankara on the Cyprus question. Other European allies generally sympathized with Turkey or adopted a neutral course; during the mid-1970s, when the United States cut aid to Turkey, the West Germans and Italians continued to provide military equipment not subject to the American ban. As a result, Turkey's closeness to these states increased dramatically. This intimacy was also based on the settlement by 1973 of nearly a million Turkish workers in Western Europe, although the workers were viewed as an mixed blessing by the Europeans.

With the advent of military rule in Turkey, relations with Western Europe became more tense. The northern European states and France displayed considerable antipathy for the ousting of a civilian regime by the generals. Rejecting the rationale for the military move in Turkey, European opinion led a number of Turkey's allies to join in pressures in the Council of Europe to penalize the Turks until they had satisfied the Europeans that their regime was truly democratic. Turkey thus strongly condemned criticial decisions reached by the Consultative Assembly of the Council of Europe after Turkey withdrew its representation in May 1981. Ankara denied allegations made by the European Council Human Rights Commission in July 1982 that Turkey had violated provisions of the Human Rights Convention. The Europeans initially seemed dissatisfied with the new Turkish constitution, and with the start-up of political party activity preceding the 1983 elections. Critical comment in Europe continued to focus on the number of parties prevented from participating in the elections and on the number of candidates vetoed by the generals shortly before election day. The Council of Europe refused to seat the parliamentarians representing Turkey in January 1984.

3.12 EURO-TURKISH PROBLEMS. Under the generals, relations with Greece suffered less than those with other European states. The Turkish military had been the element of Turkish society most interested in compromise with Greece. Hence, in the spring of 1980, the Turkish military rulers took the initiative to back away from the demand that Turkey be notified of flights in the eastern Aegean. This allowed air traffic between Greece and Turkey to resume. Similarly, late in 1980, the Turks dropped objections to the return of Greece to the military wing of NATO. But hopes of further progress were called into question by the election of Andreas Papandreou in Athens on a platform calling for a tougher line toward Turkey. The Papandreou government in power continued to voice deep suspicions of Turkey.

Another nagging problem for Turkey was the failure of European regimes to protect Turkish diplomats from Armenian terrorists. Ankara was particularly displeased at the attitude of Paris on the score. Relations with France declined to their postwar low by the early 1980s.

In this climate, Turkey was not able to engage the Europeans fully in the effort to overcome Turkish economic problems. Although Turkey had become an associate member of the European Community, the Turks found it difficult to gain the tariff privileges they believed they required for successful trade with Europe. The question of full membership in the European Communities remained in contention. As a result, Turkey found it expedient to look more to the Middle East for economic relations more seriously than it had in the past.

3.13 THE CYPRUS ISSUE. Turkish military intervention in Cyprus in 1974 divided the island, but did not bring the Greek Cypriot side to agree on a solution. In pursuit of its preferred bizonal federal solution, Turkey recognized the Turkish Federated State of Cyprus in February 1975, and began exporting mainland Turks to settle there. Ankara supported Turkish Cypriot leader Rauf Denktas in negotiations, first with Makarios and then with his successor Kyprianou representing the Greek Cypriots. Intercommunal talks have sputtered on under the auspices of the United Nations Secretary General without overcoming the major obstacles. When Denktas finally made a Unilateral Declaration of Independence in November 1983, Turkey was the only state to accord official recognition to the northern Cyprus entity. Although realizing that this step would be interpreted by the world as an acceptance of a measure of Turkish responsibility for Denktas' move, Ankara apparently felt its commitment to support the Turkish Cypriots to be too great to make any other decision. Thus the Turks accepted the possibility of disrupting relations with friends and allies as the price of loyalty to their ethnic community on the island. In order to reduce the chances of damage in its relations with the United States, however, Ankara announced a drawdown of its forces on the island as a gesture to restart negotiations with the Greek community. Denktas at the same time offered to to turn over a part of the former Greek section of Famagusta, without prejudice to final settlement, indicating that, in the Turkish Cypriot view, the declaration of independence did not preclude establishment of a confederated Cypriot state.

3.14 THE COMMUNIST WORLD. Turkey's suspicion of the Soviet Union has remained unaltered since the end of World War II. Moscow, particularly since the Cuban missile crisis of 1962, has regarded Turkey as a distinctly secondary military theater. As a result, some normalization of Turco-Soviet relations has been possible. This process was facilitated for the Turks by the Soviet stance toward

Turkey's Cyprus policies: Moscow staunchly opposed union of Cyprus with Greece. Economic cooperation between Turkey and the USSR began in the 1960s with Soviet support for selected heavy industry projects; the extent of this economic relationship was limited, however, by Moscow's unwillingness to provide more than project assistance, whereas Turkey required hard currency to meet its international obligations.

Soviet efforts to take advantage of the disruption in U.S.-Turkish relations after 1975 foundered on this same point; in addition, the government of Bulent Ecevit disregarded Moscow's appeals in 1978 not to allow the reopening of the facilities used by the United States to monitor Soviet activity when the restrictions on American military aid to Turkey were lifted. Moreover, the Soviet invasion of Afghanistan met solid disapproval in Turkey, although the Turks did not exhibit fear that this Soviet move foreshadowed greater pressure on themselves.

Soviet reaction to the regime of the generals was one of suspicion. Moscow evinced concern that Turkey would fall in with alleged U.S. plans to project military force into the Middle East. The Turkish Communist Party, based in East Germany, appealed to the Turkish populace to overthrow the "fascist junta." The Ozal government fared scarcely better in Turkish Communist eyes, although Moscow has been careful not to attack the new regime directly in order to avoid disrupting state-to-state relations.

4. PRESENT SITUATION: 1980-1984

4.1 INTERNAL - POLITICAL. On November 6, 1983 Turkey held general elections for the first civilian parliament of the third republican constitutional period. With only 45 percent of the popular vote, the Motherland Party was able to win 211 of the 400 seats. On the basis of this commanding majority, Turgut Ozal moved quickly to form his government in December 1983.

The Motherland Party prevailed in part because (1) it represented a clear break with the military regime, (2) its leader was the most seasoned political figure in the running, and (3) its economic program was seen as having promise of success. Ozal's party drew votes from across the political spectrum, but received the least support from the left-of-center constituency. Former Republican Peoples Party voters, who had no other social democratic option, appear to have provided the unexpectedly strong backing for the Populist Party, enabling it to garner 30.5 percent of the vote and 117 seats. The Nationalist Democracy Party turned in the poorest showing, dominating the voting in only four provinces in the east, and electing only 71 deputies with its 23 percent of the ballots. It seems to have been hurt by its image as an extension of the general's regime rather than an independently created organization.

Turnout was over 92 percent of the electorate, a figure considerably higher than for elections in the previous two decades of civilian rule. The elevated participation rate may have been partly induced by the imposition of a fine of 2,500 lira (less than $10, but a substantial sum for many Turks) for those who did not vote. But in the main, the high turnout probably signified the voters' interest in political stablity and a desire not to waste the chance to select the nation's leader. While the Turkish Communist Party had summoned voters in radio appeals from abroad to cast blank ballots as a protest, and rumors abounded that the banned Justice Party and Republican Peoples Party were advising the same, the number of invalid votes was not appreciably greater than in previous elections. The Social Democracy Party and the True Path Party played no part in the election, questioning whether the will of the people could be properly evaluated in view of the restricted choice available to the electorate.

Ozal used his parliamentary majority of deputies from the Motherland Party to form a government. With his commanding prestige, he was able to ignore factional differences already becoming apparent in his party in choosing the ministers. One faction of the party was composed of deputies whose background had been in the National Salvation Party of the previous era and whose religious conservatism reflected Ozal's own outlook. The other group had been drawn to the Motherland Party by Ozal's economic approach. While these two wings were soon to crystallize into competing power centers in the party, this competition did not seem significant at the start. Ozal turned to his relatives to serve in important posts, placing his brother-in-law in the key position of minister of interior.

At Ozal's direction, the Motherland Party moved quickly on the economic front to institute a broad change in the rules and incentives for the economy. He reversed protectionist measures taken after his departure from the government the previous year, and he set the economy on a course considerably more liberalization. That a government of relative newcomers to politics could act so decisively within weeks of taking office further confirmed Ozal's impressive command of the political scene.

4.2 MUNICIPAL ELECTIONS. On the political front, the Motherland Party stood up to President Evren, overturning his veto of the bill mandating early municipal elections. Ozal insisted that the Social Democracy Party and the True Path Party should be allowed to compete in these contests. This strategy appeared bold. Not only did it reverse direct rulings by the military leaders just months after their departure from power, it also offered opportunities to rival parties. These parties had considerable prospects of attracting a following from the traditional constituencies that had backed the Republican Peoples Party and the Justice Party in the previous period of civilian rule. Moving the municipal contests up to March 25, 1984, offered an advantage to the Motherland Party by reducing the time available for preparation by the new organizations. It also communicated to the electorate Ozal's impressive confidence, an attitude that commanded respect among voters.

The result of these municipal elections vindicated Ozal's political calculations and demonstrated convincingly the staying power of the Motherland Party. Candidates representing his organization swept to the mayorships in Istanbul, Ankara, and Izmir, Turkey's three largest cities, as well as in over three-quarters of the provincial capitals and over half of the remaining municipalities over the length and breadth of the country. Nationwide the party polled over 43 percent of the votes cast, proving that the drawing power of the Motherland Party had not been affected significantly by the addition of two attractive alternatives.

SODEP, under Erdal Inonu, ran second with just over 24 percent of the vote. It won in eight provincial centers and captured the mayorships in one-sixth of the other municipalities. The True Path Party came in third, collecting nearly 12 percent of the vote, although it failed to win any provincial centers and succeeded in electing mayors in only one-tenth of the municipalities. Neither the Nationalist Democracy Party nor the Populist Party were able to capture even the 10 percent of the vote that would have been necessary to collect seats had the elections been deputy contests. The NDP, however, did manage to elect mayors in three provincial capitals in the eastern part of the country where it was strong. The tiny Prosperity Party (Refah Partisi), organized since the November 1983 general elections to appeal to the former National Salvation Party constituency, was able to elect mayors in two provincial capitals, but won in only fourteen of the other municipal contests nationwide. It had been bolstered when a group of former NSP deputies joined it the month before the municipal elections. Yet its overall weak performance confirmed that it could mobilize only a fragment of the constituency of the former religious party, the rest clearly going to the Motherland Party.

Ozal interpreted the results of the municipal balloting as an endorsement of his economic policies and as a renewal of his mandate to remain in office. His liberalization program had been the main focus of campaign debate, with the opposition attacking his plan to control inflation by holding down wage increases and by restricting credit. Yet his party still won heavily, even in the poorer districts of municipalities where unemployment was rampant and wage issues were especially salient. Thus Ozal followed his impressive electoral performance in March with a wave of price increases in government-manufactured consumer items, thereby drawing bitter opposition criticism. Even some members of the Motherland

Party evinced concern over the political impact these raises could have.

The municipal elections had a major disruptive effect on the opposition. In the first place, the results undercut the emerging opposition demand for early parliamentary elections to test the mandate of the Motherland Party under conditions of broader political competition: the legitimacy of Ozal's government was resoundingly reconfirmed. Yet these opposition parties felt thoroughly vindicated in their claim that they, and not the two small parties which had deputies in parliament, were the true spokesmen for alternatives to Ozal. Hence, while SODEP in particular recognized that the populace at large was not ready for urgent demands for early elections, the two parties continued to harp on the injustice of being excluded from parliament. It was clear, therefore, that the question of early elections had been stilled only for a time, but was far from being completely resolved by the outcome of the municipal contests.

In this situation, the two major opposition formations began to put increasing pressure on the members of the small parliamentary parties to merge to produce a left-of-center and a right-of-center bloc to enhance the weight of the opposition voice in the assembly. That pressure ran up against not only the constitutional restrictions on party switching by elected deputies, but the unwillingness of the NDP and the Populist Party to abandon the political contest despite their poor showing. While the chiefs of the latter two organizations came under fire from within their own parties, conventions held following the municipal elections reconfirmed them in their leadership positions. But the continuing competition among the four major opposition parties distracted them from pursuing as vigorously as they otherwise might their attacks on the Motherland Party. Ozal's party, for its part, sought to attract to its ranks members of the Nationalist Democracy Party.

4.3 AMNESTY. Frustrated at its inability to block the Motherland Party in the new parliament, the opposition became increasingly active in appealing for public support. To curry favor with their constituencies, some civilian politicians raised the ever touchy issue of amnesty for those jailed under the military regime and for those excluded from the political competition because they had held party office in the previous era. There was ample precedent in the Turkish past for such clemency – from the Ataturk period and every decade thereafter. But the military authorities were convinced that the amnesty of terrorist suspects after the 1973 elections had been a prime factor in the rapid resumption of political violence at the end of the 1970s. Hence, Evren and others took a firm stand against letting those jailed after 1980 be released. And when some 1,200 intellectuals delivered a petition to the presidency in May 1984 calling for full human rights, including an amnesty to serve "social peace," the president told the press that "he who says he is an intellectual offends the majority." While some in the Motherland Party shared an interest in enacting some form of amnesty, the prime minister took a more cautious attitude, indicating that it should not be an early expectation. Nonetheless, agitation for an amnesty, even if not for those convicted of crimes of political violence, continued as a leitmotif in the refrain of the political opposition; it was clear that sooner or later some action would be taken on this question.

4.4 POLITICAL FRAGMENTATION. Despite the obstacles in the constitutional and legal system to a proliferation of parties, the fragmentation of the Turkish political scene continues. In addition to the Prosperity Party which achieved a modicum of success in the municipal elections, collecting nearly 5 percent of the vote in the contest for the allegiance of the conservative constituency, a Democratic Left Party has been organized to compete with SODEP and the Populist Party. By early May 1984 the Democratic Left Party claimed to have completed its organization in 23 provinces and said that thousands of members were flocking to its support. This organization advertized itself as a party on the order of the Swedish Social Democratic Party, but seemed to represent more extreme left-leaning elements than the mainstream of the Social Democracy Party. Despite its claims, the party did not appear to have a large potential constituency. It was clear that it would have an uphill fight against the better-established Populist and SODEP, although the failure of the latter's organizations to win any of the largest municipalities deprived them of valuable patronage possibilities.

4.5 MILITARY INFLUENCE. Before leaving office, the generals took great care to institute legal prohibitions against questioning the actions of the military regime. Much of the country remained under martial law, although the visible military presence had been reduced to a bare minimum during the transition to civilian government. Curfews had been lifted, and most offenses henceforth were tried in civilian, not military, courts. As evidence of their continuing political concern, the four ranking officers who had shared military rule with Evren became members of a special presidential advisory board for a six-year term under a temporary provision in the new constitution. But their authority was limited to advising the president, and they lost all executive power.

In the new structure, the scope for direct military intervention in the political realm was limited to the deliberations of the National Security Council, which dealt with security issues and no longer exercised direct political authority. Nonetheless, the armed forces continued to loom as the ultimate arbiter, to take action when other institutions failed. The prospect of arousing military disapproval has not deterred civilian politicians from activities likely to cause distress among the senior generals, such as the call for amnesty or agitation to amend the constitution to bring it more in line with the 1961 version. When President Evren spoke out against amnesty and "untimely" efforts to change the constitution, there was no doubt he was speaking for the military establishment. And when he declaimed against subversive centers attempting to recreate the banned parties of the previous civilian regime, he was again widely regarded as reflecting military concerns.

4.6 INTERNAL – ECONOMIC. It is in the economic field that Prime Minister Ozal had shown his expertise in the past. He campaigned on a platform of reducing constraints on the private sector and of creating incentives for private industry and trade. Among the major aims of his party were efforts to strengthen the middle class, reduce unemployment, provide low-cost housing, promote more balanced regional development within Turkey, and reduce bureaucratic red tape. He interpreted his party's election victories in November 1983 and March 1984 as a strong mandate to carry out this broad program of liberalization.

The initial results of the new economic measures were positive. As the government moved to devalue the currency, to approach convertibility with daily adjustments of the exchange rate, the value of the dollar on the black market fell to an insignificant premium over the bank rate. The provision to allow Turks to have foreign currency accounts for the first time in recent Turkish history reduced the need to go outside of official channels. As a result of the more realistic exchange rate and additional export incentives, export earnings rose sharply in the first months of 1984, even though some of the claimed transactions may not, in fact, have taken place. The improvement in the balance of payments was favorably received by the international banking community.

Despite initial signs of progress, the debate on economic policy did not abate. Spokesmen of opposing parties expressed doubts that sufficient foreign exchange would be forthcoming from exports and remittances to meet Turkey's requirmeents. Fears were expressed that the country's reserves of $2 billion would be exhausted in short order. The opposition expecially derided Ozal's plan, which he pushed through parliament over their strong objections, to allow private investors to buy shares in public sector enterprises such as the Bosporus bridge. Complaints were raised that government employees and others on fixed incomes were being squeezed by rising costs of imported goods, thereby imparting a new fillip to the exodus of the more talented from the bureaucracy into private industry. Government-imposed wage restraint was not popular, especially as inflation remained well above the target of a 25 percent increase per annum.

Despite Ozal's overall progress in combatting the ills of the Turkish economy, unemployment and an inability to speed the creation of new jobs continue to plague Turkey. To cope with these challenges, the new economic policies include tax reduction on savings in an effort to promote investment and heavy taxation of luxury consumption to discourage unnecessary imports. Increased credit is allocated to farmers and artisans in order to slow the influx to the cities by stimulating new opportunities in the small towns and villages. While the aim of such measures is to energize the domestic economy, it will take some time to test their effectiveness.

4.7 EXTERNAL. The Ozal government introduced no new notes into Turkish foreign policy. It pushed hard in its effort to gain acceptance by the Europeans for Turkey's refurbished policial order, sending parliamentarians to the Council of Europe and threatening to "sever totally" relations with that body if it persisted in rejecting Turkish representatives. This tough stance, coupled with the convincing demonstration in the municipal elections that even in broader political competition the Ozal government was representative of public opinion in Turkey, put the European critics on the defensive; Turkey thus regained its seats in the Council without compromising the anti-terrorist measures it considers necessary for internal security.

Known for his interest in the Islamic world, Ozal stressed that close ties with the Arab and Islamic states were considered complementary to relationships with Europe. In line with this approach, the first foreign trip that Ozal announced was to Iran to cement current bonds and to conclude major new trade deals. He followed up with early visits to Iraq and Libya, also among the states with the largest trade with Turkey. The weight of economic factors made this orientation logical, but Ozal's personal enthusiasm to penetrate Middle Eastern markets was evident in his public emphasis on such activity.

Relations with the United States remained the anchor of Turkey's foreign policy structure. Although some concern was expressed by Turks over possibly differing emphasis in strategic view with regard to American plans to develop rapid deployment forces for the Middle East, this issue appeared to remain within manageable proportions. Turkey allowed the Multinational Force in Lebanon, composed of a U.S., UK, Italian, and French contingent, to be supported through Turkish facilities, although there was evident relief among the Turks when that arrangement lapsed after the withdrawal of the Multinational Force early in 1984. Clearly, Turkey's military establishment valued the strategic relationship with the United States; the willingness of successive American administrations to give priority to aid to Turkey and the relatively high level of this aid provided a solid base for cooperation. Thus, although Congressional unhappiness at Turkey for recognizing the unilateral declaration of independence by the Turkish Cypriots in November 1983 led to moves by the U.S. Senate and House to trim Reagan Administration military aid requests for Turkey, the overall aid package still had enough of value to temper Turkish feelings of disappointment. Exchanges of visits by senior officials emphasized the persisting intimacy of the relationship.

The Reagan Administration support was all the more welcome in Ankara in view of Turkey's problems with its European allies. The Ozal regime reacted with interest rather than pique to the plan announced by President Reagan in May 1984 to establish a $250 million Peace and Reconstruction fund for Cyprus. This fund was to be released to the parties when "real progress" had been recorded in reducing Turkish troop strength on the island or in turning over the city of Famagusta to the United Nations for resettlement by the Greek Cypriots. In accepting this approach, the American Congress moved to reduce the Reagan Administration's aid request for Turkey by $85 million to $670 million for 1984, a figure the Turkish government reluctantly accepted.

Management of the Greek and Cypriot policies of the Ankara regime formed the final major strand of Turkey's foreign relationships. Ozal took office with appeals to Greece to engage in bilateral negotiations and called the Cypriots to dialogue with the self-declared Turkish Republic of Northern Cyprus. But as a result of the recognition of the northern Cyprus regime by his military predecessors only weeks before, he faced uphill sledding in reassuring the Greeks. Waters were further oiled when Ankara announced in April 1984 that it was exchanging ambassadors with northern Cyprus, a state that had not gained recognition by any other nation in the six months of its existence. The exchange of ambassadors, which further complicated continuing UN efforts to promote a negotiating process, provoked new objections from the Hellenic world. In this there seemed little prospect that the return to civilian rule in Ankara would overcome the obstacles that had long frustrated progress in improving relations between Turkey and its Greek neighbors. As long as the Cyprus problem remains unresolved, the prospect that this tortured issue could upset Turkey's whole alliance structure remains real.

5. PROSPECTS

5.1 NEW STRUCTURES. Turkey's new political structure was designed to prevent a recurrence of the problems of the past by detailed remedies. The constitution is configured to address the circumstances of political paralysis, threats to the integrity of the state from within, and derogation from the secular reform approach associated with Ataturk. These were the chief impediments to the smooth functioning of elected parliamentary democracy as diagnosed by the military rulers and by many civilians as well. The constitution does not rely on general prescriptions to be interpreted as new challenges arise. Turkish politicians seem more comfortable with applying specific formulations than in following general principles in their fundamental legislation. Thus it is to the extent that the problems of the future resemble those of the past that the new regime can be expected to operate more or less effectively.

Written instruments make a difference in Turkey: the Turks take seriously the provisions of law and treaties. It is precisely because legal documents are observed that a constitution must be followed to the letter or thrown out entirely. In the Turkish context, basic laws cannot be ignored. Thus the next few years will see a breaking-in period for the constitution as politicians seek to adapt to the new structure.

The constitutional solutions embodied in the present system are inherently long-term and are by no means "quick fixes." The carefully balanced set of rewards to assure that the largest party is overrepresented in parliament while minor factions get no seats if they fall below the national threshold may have prevented Ozal from having to seek coalition partners, to the relief of the senior generals. But these provisions have not stopped fragmentation of the political scene. As long as ambitious individuals are thrown up in the process of political competition, the inclination to form additional parties is likely to be strong, even if the newcomers appear to have little chance of long-range success. At least until after the next general elections due in 1988, the political scene is assured of remaining fragmented as the current crop of parties assert their claims to represent a significant portion of the electorate.

Despite the failure of the system to meet the immediate expectations of its framers in reducing party proliferation, the Turks have made impressive progress in returning to civilian politics. Major decision-making power has returned to the party politicians. While Prime Minisiter Ozal and President Evren continue to work out ambiguities in the prescriptions for meshing their respective prerogatives and powers, including such contentious issues as the right to appoint senior administrators, the civilian side appears to be in the ascendant. For example, Evren seems unable to get regional governates established over the opposition of the Motherland Party.

Ozal has conspicuous latitude in ordering economic policy. As long as the results are not disastrous, his economic departures, however radical, will not meet political or extralegal prohibitions. He may encounter bureaucratic footdragging from a civil service with deep traditions of hostility to private enterprise and the free market, but control of the majority party is sufficient to carry out his policy.

In political matters, the equities may be more complex. Questions of foreign policy are hemmed in by existing treaties and international engagements. Key relationships, especially those with the United States, intrude into a domain where the interests of the military establishment must be taken into serious consideration. Similarly, matters such as the scope and timing of amnesties for those jailed during the period of military rule are issues to be sorted out, not only with the leadership of the armed forces, but with the political parties inside and outside of parliament as well. Ozal's commitment to gradual reduction of the areas under martial law falls under the concern with national security which the constitution dictates will be shared with the military leaders. Give and take among the parties to work out in practice the legal limits on political activity will evolve over time. All elements of the Turkish polity are likely to become involved in reaching this accommodation. The bottom line is that the civilian leaders and not the military are now the arbiters of these important processes.

Turkey's recent experiences raise the question of how committed the military establishemnt is to letting civilians work out their political destiny. In judging the answer, it is useful to recognize that the disengagement of the armed forces from the political scene is a theme that runs deep through modern Turkish history. Ataturk set parliamentary democracy as the norm for governing the country. There is general acceptance within all institutions in Turkey that only in exceptional circumstances can this system be suspended. Thus, having erected a structure that appeared to answer the need for more effective government without permitting one-party tyranny, the military establishment itself recognized that the time had come to resume parliamentary rule. Barring an unforeseen catastrophe, the armed forces are almost certain to hold to this decision. The prospect is for increasing military disengagement rather than for the ranking generals to remain involved in the political process.

5.2 CHALLENGES Over the longer run, there are two main sets of circumstances that could alter this picture. Turkey's rulers are aware of these menaces and are on their guard to fend them off. First, moves to broaden the political contest beyond the limits of current laws and constitution would pose a powerful provocation to the military leadership. Such moves could come from a number of directions. The leaders of the banned major parties are clearly unhappy at their prohibition from reentering the political arena for the next decade. Efforts by them, either directly or through a facade, to resume political activity would roil the political waters. If such a challenge were not resisted successfully by the civilian politicians, the affront to the military could provoke the senior generals to end this initiative.

A similar challenge by doctrinaire leftists and/or proto-fascists to create their own organizations in defiance of prohibitions on such activity would be even more destabilizing. More likely, such elements might seek to push existing legal political organizations toward the extremes, presenting a threat that might be difficult for civilian politicians to handle. The legal provisions permitting overseas Turks to vote almost inevitably will, in the long run, foster more extreme political views within Turkey; the large Turkish population in West Germany is subject to intensive propaganda from the illegal Turkish Communist Party, based in East Germany, and from the banned National Action Party of Alparslan Turks, which continues outside its Anatolian homeland. Although such extremist activity is not likely to prove successful in the short run, any progress by the left or right to regain political legitimacy could generate a response from the military leaders. Of course, a recrudescence of politically-motivated terrorism in conjunction with this ideological agitation would pose an immediate provocation to the armed forces. Continuing arrests of members of dissident organizations with caches of arms indicate that terrorism is merely under control, not eliminated. Should terrorists score spectacular strikes, the prestige of civilian government would be sorely undermined and the pressure for military intervention would rise accordingly.

The second general line of development that would increase the chances of military involvement in politics would be a failure of the present political structure to provide effective government. Coalition politics marked the preceding constitutional period; at that time, the parties showed themselves incapable of cooperating even against strong domestic challenges to national security. If, as a result of the fragmentation of the political scene, a need for coalition government should again arise, it would be essential that the political bargaining to form such a cabinet be accomplished without delay and bring into being an administration able to act decisively. If not, the political system would be at risk. Even should a single party manage to win a parliamentary majority, a certain level of cooperation in across party lines is needed for the efficient functioning of the regime. Persistent calls for early elections, or even threats by the majority party to move up the election date as a means to keep the minor parties in line, contribute to a constant campaign atmosphere; this could erode the effectiveness of a government with a strong parliamentary majority. Thus, as in any democratic system, there is a high premium on the establishment of the concept of loyal opposition, a notion that has not heretofore taken deep root in Turkey. The smooth functioning of a parliamentary system requires greater willingness to sublimate partisan interest for the general good than Turkish political leaders have customarily shown in the past. The level of rhetoric and the intensity of personal invective since the start of political activity before the 1983 elections is not reassuring in this regard.

5.3 POLITICAL PATTERNS. Among the more hopeful auguries for the continuing health of the Turkish polity, are the indications that the division of the electorate into a left-of-center and a right-of-center constituency has persisted into the current constitutional period. It seems inevitable that in time the bulk of each constituency will fall into line behind a major party; Turkish voters in the past have displayed a consistent tendency to jump on the bandwagon of the winning party. Even with rules favoring the persistence of splinter parties in the second republican period, minor parties lost ground in each successive election after their initial appearance on the political stage. We cannot yet tell how long the new process of shakedown will take before the emergence of two rival organizations. Although Ozal enjoys a definite advantage, it is by no means assured that he and his Motherland Party, for all their successes thus far, will be able to solidify their hold on the center against their rivals. Indeed, Ozal appears to face more powerful competition for the allegiance of the right-of-center constituency, in the contest with the True Path Party and the tiny Prosperity Party, than does Inonu for the left-of-center voters, against the challenge of the Populist Party and the Democratic Left Party.

Which party will capture the center-right constituency is undoubtedly bound up with the success of Ozal's economic policies. If his intense free market orientation does produce an acceptable level ot economic stability and a return to high rates of growth, he has an excellent chance to stabilize his party's position as the dominant force in Turkish politics. But if recovery should falter, Ozal's leadership would come under question and his party's popularity could decline. In this event, a Justice Party-oriented successor would be likely to win the allegiance of enough of the center-right voters to knock the Motherland Party out of first place. That would in turn offer an opportunity to SODEP, which faces little opposition in its quest to replace the old Republican Party as the favorite of those to the left of center, to gain a plurality, if not a majority, in parliament. In this situation, Turkey might revert to a more social-democratic approach to economics, with an expanded public sector. But Inonu has expressed no interest in altering the export incentives that have contributed to the vitality of that sector.

5.4 SOCIAL PROBLEMS. The task of creating a new political structure – albeit formidable – has been easier than the concomitant work of resolving the country's social and economic problems. The strains of development are certain to dog Turkey for a long time to come. An increasingly mobile population will present a constant challenge under restored democratic procedures. Economic success, leading to some reduction of the present high rates of unemployment and underemployment, is clearly necessary if social tensions are to be alleviated over the longer run. Greater attention to raising development rates in the less-advantaged regions of Turkey is also essential to diminish the sense of grievance that has propelled Kurds and others into leftist violence in the past. Faster development rates in the eastern provinces can contribute to slowing the pace of urbanization, vitally necessary if Turkey's cities are to remain manageable over the long term. The economic stabilization program has yet to alleviate problems of this sort; indeed, with its insistence on restraining wage increases, the program is adding to the difficulties of the workers. Labor pressure is thus likely to grow, and strikes may again become an important problem. Turk-Is is already pushing harder than the regime finds comfortable on bread-and-butter labor issues. Hence, unless and until the root causes that have disrupted social cohesion and promoted political violence in the past are attenuated, the Turkish democratic system will remain vulnerable and on trial.

III. ECONOMIC ANALYSIS

1. SUMMARY CONCLUSIONS

1.1 RESOURCES. Many of Turkey's resources continue to be underdeveloped. Government efforts are underway to encourage foreign investment for the development of the country's mineral wealth. Turkish agriculture remains relatively inefficient, although agricultural productivity has increased. Industrial growth was negative in the late seventies, and has grown moderately since. Tourism, in spite of its high potential, yields Turkey a relatively small income.

1.2 RECENT POLITICAL DEVELOPMENTS. The economic crisis of 1977-79 was caused by the oil price shocks, an overvalued exchange rate, fiscal pressures, and political instability. This resulted in huge current account deficits, high inflation and foreign debt, and very slow growth, particularly in industry. The situation improved in the early eighties, with the return to political stability, although the pressure in the labor market (reflected in high unemployment and underemployment), and the financial crisis of 1982, have threatened Turkey's recovery. Ozal's election has restored a measure of stability; his identification with the middle class was taken as a reassuring sign by business circles.

1.3 ENERGY. Turkey continues to be seriously dependent on foreign oil imports, being able to produce only 15 percent of its needs. Exploration has revealed that Turkey has little chance of producing vast amounts of oil cheaply. However, considerable potential exists in the use of coal, lignite, and hydroelectric power. Even if these resources are fully developed, however, experts doubt that Turkey will be self-sufficient in energy.

1.4 INDUSTRY. The crisis of 1977-79 slowed the rate of industrial growth considerably. The situation improved dramatically after the military takeover owing to the inflow of foreign exchange and the improvement in labor relations. Capacity utilization has risen steadily and markedly since 1980. The share of investment goods in industrial production has been growing at the expense of consumer goods in the past two decades.

1.5. AGRICULTURE. The relative importance of agriculture in GDP and in employment has been declining, owing to the government's erstwhile inward-oriented development strategy and growing industrialization. The agricultural sector is still important, however. Agriculture continues to be inefficient, although better technology has improved yields and reduced dependence on climatic conditions.

1.6 CONSTRUCTION. Construction has been seriously hurt by the recession in Turkey and worldwide. It is still an important sector, and Turkey plays a major role in construction in the Middle East and Africa. Contracts obtained abroad provide employment for Turks and result in higher remittances from workers and companies.

1.7 BALANCE OF PAYMENTS. Higher oil prices and an overvalued lira led to huge current account deficits in the late seventies. The deficit has since narrowed, as oil prices have fallen and exports (especially to other Middle Eastern states) have grown rapidly; the lira has been devalued twice. Import payments are expected to continue to grow, but exports should also maintain a high growth rate. The prognosis is for a smaller current account deficit – barring a major increase in oil prices. The debt service ratio should also decline somewhat.

1.8 FINANCIAL SECTOR. The budget deficit has been brought under control as the result of a major tax reform in 1981. Monetary growth has also been curbed, reducing inflation but slowing economic growth. The banking sector experienced a crisis in 1982, which was contained by swift government action.

2. MACRO-ECONOMIC ANALYSIS

2.1 RECENT DEVELOPMENTS, 1962 - 1982. The Turkish economy performed well during the first three five-year plan periods (1962-77). It achieved an average of 6.5 percent annual GNP growth during these 15 years. Sectoral growth rates were distinctly important: roughly 3 percent in agriculture, 9.5 percent in industry, and 7.5 percent in services and construction. In the face of a 2.5 percent population increase, the 6.5 percent income growth allowed per capita real GNP to expand by 4 percent. The slightly more than 3 percent agricultural income growth made Turkey self-sufficient in food and able to export certain agricultural products.

Many elements contributed to the economic crisis of 1977-79: the 1973 and 1979 oil price shocks, a late policy response to the oil shocks, an overvalued exchange rate, a budget deficit caused by heavy investment expenditures, weak coalition governments, political instability and ensuing anarchy. This resulted in a high foreign debt, an inability to pay for imports, and high inflation. On January 24, 1980, with a sharp policy change, Turkey inaugurated an IMF-type stabilization program, which enabled her to reduce the inflation rate from 100 percent in 1980 to 40 percent in 1981, and around 30 percent in 1982, while exports rose from about $2.5 billion in 1980 to $4.2 billion and $5.7 billion in 1981 and 1982, respectively. Furthermore, there was a modest rise in the volume of imports: $7.4, $8.2 and $8.8 billion for 1980, 1981 and 1982, respectively. During the same years, the current account balance deficit was reduced from a peak of $-3.2 billion in 1980 to $-2.1 billion in 1981 and $-1.2 billion in 1982.

In the 1977-82 period, Turkey's real GNP growth averaged around 2 percent. Sectoral growth rates were 2.4 percent in agriculture, 1 percent in industry, and 2.4 percent in services. In short, Turkey's stabilization experience constitutes a success story among the several similar stabilization programs all over the world.

2.2 RECENT MACRO-ECONOMIC PERFORMANCE. The 1962-77 period was marked by a redoubled effort to promote industrialization through an import-substitution strategy. In fact, an average 9.5 percent real income growth and nearly 4 percent employment growth was achieved in the industrial sector during this period. Internal terms of trade have favored industry. This is reflected in a comparison of sectoral GDP shares based on national income data calculated from time series figures in current prices as opposed to the ones in constant prices.

Structural Changes in GDP

	in current prices			in 1968 prices		
Sectors	**1962**	**1977**	**1982**	**1962**	**1977**	**1982**
Agriculture	39.4	27.6	20.7	38.1	23.1	23.4
Industry	16.1	19.8	27.7	15.4	23.6	22.3
Services & Construction	44.5	52.5	51.6	46.5	53.3	54.3
G.D.P.	100.0	100.0	100.0	100.0	100.0	100.0

In 1968 prices, the share of industry had risen from about 15 percent in 1962 to around 23 percent in the 1977-82 period, while the share of agriculture dropped from 38 23 percent. The more dramatic rise of the share of industry from 16 to nearly 28 percent when calculated from current price data, reflects the high degree of protection accorded to the industrial sector.

The above picture conceals a considerable increase in the <u>per laborer value added</u> levels in those three sectors. In fact, the per laborer productivity figure almost doubled in agriculture and services and increased almost two and a half times in industry during the 1962-82 period.

Labor Productivity Levels
(Value Added Per Laborer)
1982 prices

Sectors	1962	1977	1982
Agriculture	93.5	153.1	173.8
Industry	494.3	1167.0	1192.4
Services & Construction	577.2	886.5	913.2
National Average	196.9	457.0	493.1

2.3 MACRO-ECONOMIC RESOURCES AND EXPENDITURES, 1962-1982. The period 1962-1982 saw a number of far-reaching macro-economic developments, many of which have had a lasting impact on the structure of the Turkish economy.

Foreign Deficit. During the first two five-year plan periods (1962-72), Turkey achieved a high degree of discipline in the area of foreign (current account) deficit. During these years, on average the foreign deficit was around 2 percent of GNP.

In contrast, the foreign deficit reached 13 percent during the 1972-77 period, fell to 8.8 percent in 1978 and was close to 5 percent during the 1979-82 period. The main culprit for this rise in the foreign deficit was the 1973 oil shock and a delay in policy response to it. Another factor was the high import requirement of the "import substitution industries," which were favored before 1980 to the detriment of export activities. For the year 1982, the foreign deficit stood at 2.2 percent of GNP.

Investments. Total investments were about 15 percent of the GNP in 1962. During the first two plan periods they were raised to 18.4 and 21 percent. During the 1972-77 period, adherence to a cheap energy policy, the continuation of high levels of worker remittances, and the accumulation of foreign debts enabled Turkey to achieve a 24 percent investment rate. Since this policy was obviously not sustainable, investments fell to around 20 percent for the 1978-82 period.

The share of the private sector in total investments was around 47-48 percent during the first ten years, rising to 52 percent in 1973-78, and falling to 42 percent in the 1979-82 period.

Total consumption. Total consumption grew around 4-5 percent from 1962 to 1972, and jumped to a high of 6.9 percent during 1973-77. It was about zero in 1978, and fell to a low of -0.4 percent as an average for the 1979-82 period. It registered positive growth rates of 0.6 for 1981 and 4.2 percent for 1982. In the meantime, per capita consumption was 4.4 percent for 1973-77, and fell to 2.6 percent in the 1979-82 period.

Prices and costs. Turkey has not had a history of high inflation. During the 1962-77 period, the CPI and WPI registered the following average yearly increases for the three five-year plan periods: roughly 6 percent for the first, 10 percent for the second, and 17 percent for the third.

In 1979, 1980 and 1981, however, inflation reached 65, 100, and 40 percent levels, respectively. The rate of inflation was close to 30 percent for 1982 (29.6 percent for Istanbul).

During the second half of 1982, financial market troubles and subsequent rescue operation were important events, negatively affecting economic stability. Furthermore, domestic oil prices, tied to a strong U.S. dollar, continued to cause cost-push domestic inflation. In the meantime, a distinctly moderate wage increase policy contributed to checking the cost increases since 1980; real wages declined by 25.3 percent in 1980, and by 7.3 percent in 1981; they grew a mere 1 percent in 1982.

On the other hand, measures to reduce costs through rationalizing the industrial organization structure, both in the public sector (the State Economic Enterprises) and private industry, continue to be a major area of concern in Turkey.

Labor surplus. The Turkish economy has a dualistic structure. This is reflected in the fact that about 9.5 million people out of an active population of 15.5 million are employed in agriculture. About 665,000 people, roughly 7 percent of the 9.5 million working in agriculture, are estimated to experience disguised unemployment. On top of that, another 2.2 million people are estimated to be in the non-agricultural surplus labor category.

Thus the total surplus labor is estimated to be roughly 2.8 million people, or 16 percent of the civilian labor supply.

Out of this 2.8 million surplus labor only 900,000 are actively seeking work. The remaining large group consists of 1.2 million discouraged workers who do not seek work, and the 665,000 underemployed in agriculture.

Furthermore, out of 900,000 only about 450,000 people who seek work through the Public Employment Services are registered unemployed.

The dualistic structure of the economy creates this rather variegated grouping of surplus labor because the labor market cannot be expected to have the same degree of transparency as in a mature industrialized economy. Nevertheless, it may be more appropriate to take only the non-agricultural surplus ratio, which is about 12 percent for 1982 and 1983 for cross-country comparisons. This ratio was less than 6 percent until 1972 and doubled during the second part of the 1972-82 period.

Even if we concentrate on the larger ratio of 16 percent surplus labor for 1982 and 1983, we can say that the characteristics of the unemployment situation are quite different in Turkey than in other OECD countries. As there is no formal unemployment insurance system in Turkey, the extended tamily system continues to act as a non-official unemployment insurance scheme. In addition, the government sector has acted as an employer of the last resort to many who could not find employment.

Since the inauguration of the stabilization program, however, total government sector employment, including the State Economic Enterprises, has stood constant at around 2 million people.

2.4 POLICY ISSUES AND INSTITUTIONAL CHANGES. A major policy change occurred in Turkey in 1980 in the form of the economic stabilization program. A series of decontrols gave increasing weight to market mechanism. The policy instituted a switch to export orientation as opposed to the strict import substitution strategy of the past three decades, especially for those foreign investments which help promote exports, and a distinctly liberal turn in policies on foreign capital. Trade-related international relations have also been eagerly pursued since 1980. These efforts have recently been extended to the Near and Far East.

A series of sweeping institutional changes has been instituted since the September 12, 1980, military coup which ended the rampant anarchy and terrorism that had raged in the country during a succession of weak coalition governments. These changes include such amendments to the political-legal framework as a new constitution, a new law on political parties, and an election law. There are changes to the economic legal framework, in tax law, labor relations and collective bargaining law, banking and financial markets, as well as social changes like the creation of new arrangements for education, birth control, and the provision of health services in general.

These far-reaching institutional changes are expected to put Turkey on a higher economic, social, and political development track, provided that the reform efforts are pursued in accordance with the shifting exigencies and rapid changes facing Turkey at home and abroad. The commitment to accepting this challenge seems complete and performance since 1980 is promising.

2.5 1983 BASE PERIOD. As is typically the case with any stabilization program, difficulties occurred in the financial markets during the second half of 1982. These difficulties were largely contained by a rescue operation arranged by the Central Bank and the Ministry of Finance, which entailed the Treasury taking over the ailing Hisarbank and Istanbul Bankasi. Efforts to improve the state of the financial markets and to secure higher efficiency are continuing.

Another important area of concern is the labor market. The rate of population growth, which was about 2.5 percent during the 1962-77 period, declined to 2.2 percent during the 1977-82 economic crisis. However, even this reduced rate implies great pressure on the labor market, in the face of reduced growth at home and diminished prospects for Turkish workers to find employment in Western Europe.

In short, in 1981 and 1982 there were difficulties in the financial and labor markets. Furthermore, increasing protectionist tendencies, especially in the EEC area, and severe competition elsewhere plagued the economy.

Higher performance. Turkey enjoys a satisfactory atmosphere for higher production and export performance. This is reflected in a high degree of determination to maintain budgetary discipline, a favorable attitude towards domestic and foreign private entrepreneurial initiatives, a distinct moderation in wage increases, and effective as of July 1983, 5 percent reduction in the interest rates.

Furthermore, Turkey, unlike many other countries in the Near East, possesses relatively well-trained middle and high-level manpower, a comparatively large potential domestic market, considerable natural resources and infrastructure vital for economic development.

When contrasted with most cases in Latin American and Eastern Block countries, the rather successful management of the 1980 stabilization program raised Turkey's credit worthiness considerably.

Indicators. The major economic indicators for 1983 indicate modest success for the economic program introduced by the military. The Gross National Product grew at 3.3 percent, which is fairly impressive in view of economic stagnation world-wide and the highly conservative mood of international financial institutions. The industrial sector recorded the highest growth rate: 6.4 percent, increasing its share of GDP slightly. Wholesale and retail trade grew by 6.2 percent, and transport and communications by 2.8 percent. Other sectors recorded low growth rates: construction grew 0.8 percent, financial institutions 0.5 percent. Agriculture declined by 0.2 percent. These developments reflect a very modest recovery spearheaded by industrial investment, which continues its upward trend, raising the proportion of GDP accounted for by industry. At the same time, the service sector is growing more slowly, while agriculture continues to decline.

Factor income from abroad in 1983 is reported to have fallen by 66.2 percent in terms of current prices, and 74.8 percent in terms of fixed prices. This is the result of lower workers' remittances from abroad, higher foreign debt service payments as a result of higher interest rates world-wide, and a higher rate of profit repatriation by foreign companies operating in Turkey in response to a law facilitating such transfers.

Inflation remains relatively high; the Ministry of Commerce estimates the inflation rate for the twelve months ending in November, 1983 to have been 39.9; the Istanbul Chamber of Commerce has estimated a 34.3 percent rate for the corresponding period. This does not, of course, reflect the consequences of the policies of the new government, but it highlights the magnitude of the problems facing the government as it seeks to appease the international financial community through austerity measures.

2.6 SHORT- AND MEDIUM-TERM PROSPECTS. It is not impossible that Turkey will achieve a 6 percent GDP growth with a reasonable price stability of about 15 percent in the near future. With such growth performance, Turkey may be able to create new productive jobs for about 1.2 to 1.4 million people in the next five years, keeping its surplus labor ratio around the present level. It is hoped that this economic development will be facilitated by an increasingly liberalized world trade and finance environment. In other words, this high growth prospect requires a satisfactory degree of cooperation from Turkey's development partners, who must resist further protectionism toward Turkish exports, and avoid a forced mass return of Turkish workers presently employed in Western Europe. In addition, it demands joint-venture developmental operations, and the sharing of technology, know-how, and financial resources, at home and in markets abroad.

An annual GDP growth rate of 5 percent may be more realistic through 1988, barring major oil price increases. A 7 percent growth rate is feasible thereafter. Fixed investment seems set to grow 6-7 percent annually, so that fixed investment will rise as a percentage of GDP from 19.6 percent currently to 22 percent in 1990, making healthy GDP growth possible. This prognosis assumes a growth of exports of 7-8 percent, which would be equal to or slightly greater than the growth rate of imports, assuming no drastic oil price increases.

On that basis, it is likely that imports of goods as a percentage of GDP (currently 13.6) will remain higher than exports of goods as a percentage of GDP (currently 10.5). Conservative projections suggest that in 1990 imports will constitute 16 percent of GDP, while exports will constitute slightly less than 13 percent. This should cause the current account deficit to narrow, but will probably not eliminate it altogether. Even a modest escalation in oil prices would cause the current account deficit to increase as a percentage of GDP. It is likely that Turkey's debt service ratio will decline from its current level of 24.2 percent to a more manageable 20 percent in 1990, or even 15 percent if oil prices remain stable and export growth is robust.

A major imponderable, however, is the possibility of renewed labor unrest. It must be remembered that the "social peace" achieved by the junta entailed the virtual suppression of organized labor. Furthermore, business confidence has been restored through the intimidation of workers and the arbitrary reduction of industrial wages. A potential for labor unrest clearly exists, although it is likely to depend, to a large extent, on the length of the public memory of the time of chaos (prior to the 1980 coup). That memory is what has occasioned the passive acceptance of the restraints that have been implemented. As it begins to fade, however, dissatisfaction with economic conditions may become a paramount consideration, circumventing Turkey's long-awaited recovery.

The IMF and the international financial community, taking courage from Turkey's recent and continuing stabilization experience, have a supportive approach to Turkey's development efforts, as evidenced by the recent extension of credit to Turkey.

2.7 ECONOMIC POLICY MAKING, STATISTICAL DATA, RESEARCH BASE. The Turkish economy has followed a mixed economic policy. Since the 1961 Constitution, the economic and social development of the country has been conducted within the framework of official development plans. The plan is predictive for the private sector and prescriptive for the public sector.

The public sector accounts for roughly half of total investments and is active in energy, in many sub-sectors of the manufacturing industry, and in a large part of transportation, and financial institutions. During the troubled years of the 1930s, the State Economic Enterprises (SEE) were established out of sheer necessity in the face of world recession, crisis and inadequate accumulation of private capital and entrepreneurship at home.

Indeed, the SEEs did help to establish most basic heavy and intermediate industry, as well as mass production of basic wage goods through successful import substitution. After the Second World War, the private sector achieved tremendous accumulation of capital and established itself in nearly all branches of economic activity. Since 1980, the policy gives more weight to market forces and assigns a greater role to private economy through a wide variety of incentives. Nevertheless, the public sector still has a vital responsibility in achieving the targets of the economic plans.

The prospective plans of 15 years are drawn up as a framework for the five-year development plans. Technically, the plans are based on consistency models that try to establish satisfactory coordination between various tasks and available means. Yearly programs are prepared under the five-year plan. These yearly programs contain an evaluation of past and present trends of various detailed targets, and implementation results for many sectors and sub-sectors, including social sectors like education, health, housing. They indicate the policy measures envisaged, and contain separate volumes, spelling out incentives provided to private sector investors by industry and by geographical regions. In fact, these yearly economic programs constitute the basis of the central government's fiscal budget. Furthermore, monetary and financial aspects of the economy are closely coordinated through a special committee at the Prime Ministerial level with the participation of the Minister of Finance, the Governor of the Central Bank, and the head of the State Planning Organization, among others.

Although statistical data collection and economic research activities have been important programs since the advent of formal development planning in 1960, there is urgent need for overhauling the existing data collection arrangements and research base.

3. PLANNING AND PUBLIC POLICY

3.1 ECONOMIC DEVELOPMENT PROGRAM. Since 1961, Turkey has been engaged in efforts to plan its economic development. The State Planning Organization, set up in that year, has drawn up a series of five-year development plans, which are prescriptive for state economic activity, but only descriptive as regards the course of the private sector. The Fourth Five-Year Plan, adopted in 1978, called for raising the GNP ($1,130 per capita) by 8 percent annually through 1983 by encouraging agriculture as well as industrial development; it reflected the growing emphasis on promoting exports. Earlier plans had been more heavily weighted toward industry, particularly favoring import substitution enterprises. The current plan envisages infrastructure expansion, especially upgrading the electric power grid and generating capacity. While the overall plan soon became outdated by Turkey's intense economic crisis, annual supplements have attempted to make adjustments to conform to the program agreed upon in 1980 with the International Monetary Fund and with other international lenders to stabilize Turkey's economy.

Turkey's stabilization and economic recovery program, now into its fifth year of application, has yielded the intended results. This is the more remarkable as the world economy has been in prolonged recession, accompanied by rising protectionism and retrenchment in international financing as an increasing number of developing and Eastern Block countries seek to reschedule their foreign debts. In 1982, while the OECD-area GNP stagnated and the balance of payments of many countries became major policy concerns, the GNP in Turkey increased by 4 percent and the external deficit was substantially reduced. The inflation rate was also lowered further.

The guidelines of the forthcoming Five Year Plan have been released. They call, among other things, for cutting inflation to 25 percent, and obtaining membership in the EEC – a problematic goal, in view of the opposition of certain EEC members. The guidelines also indicate continued support for the "mixed economy" approach, allowing enough free enterprise to stimulate growth and please the international financial community, while maintaining the public sector to avoid reliquishing control over the direction of the economy to independent forces or alienating the two million people employed by the state bureaucracy who are the mainstay of Ozal's support.

3.2 PUBLIC AND PRIVATE SECTOR. Throughout the period of state planning, the share of the private sector in total investment varied between 42 percent and 52 percent. However, the predominance of state economic enterprises in the developed portion of Turkey's economy has been decreasing in recent years. The state sector still bulks so large that the inefficiences of state economic enterprises, which are charged with important social welfare roles, impose a drag on development. A major concern of the 1980 reform program, agreed upon with the International Monetary Fund, was to put the state economic enterprises on a pay-as-you-go basis. That meant huge rises in the prices of goods and a large reduction in the advantage that these enterprises enjoy over private competitors.

3.3 BUDGET. Budget deficits and deficit financing through the Central Bank, which increases the supply of money, are generally held responsible for generating inflationary pressures. After the inflationary process starts and gains momentum, budget expenditures tend to adjust to inflation faster than budget revenues. Until the end of 1980, this had been the case in Turkey. In 1981, however, a sharp turnaround occurred in Turkey's public finances with the implementation of a major tax refom.

The consolidated budget, which includes the accounts of the central government and the annexed budgets of several government agencies, showed a net deficit of $500 million in 1979 which increased sharply to $1.1 billion in 1980. As a result, the net borrowing requirement of the consolidated budget increased from $200 million in 1979 to $1 billion in 1980. In 1981, a large increase in revenues led to a decrease in the net deficit to $200 million, which in turn reduced the net borrowing requirement to $400 million, down 57.2 percent from the previous year's level.

The availability of final budget data is usually delayed about two years, making the formulation of budget targets for the coming fiscal year difficult since only very approximate estimates of the budget of the current period are known. This is of particular importance at times of high inflation and when changes in tax legislation are being considered.

In the past, matters were further complicated by the government's power to (1) increase budget appropriations, (as in the case of salary increases for civil servants granted in the course of the fiscal year), and (2) borrow short term from the Central Bank up to 15 percent of total appropriations.

3.4 MONITORING. Close monitoring of the cash flow by the treasury has been essential to ensure that budgets are kept within the permitted limits. A major improvement was the decision to abolish most subsidies to loss-making state enterprises and to require the latter to increase prices and cut costs. This not only led to a less distorted price structure but also contributed to a gradual improvement in the finances of these enterprises. There is, however, still reason for concern. For 1983, it was decided not to resort to "automatic" appropriations increases.

Delays in the collation of final budget data make an analysis of fiscal policy in 1982 and 1983 difficult. Nevertheless, it appears that the 1982 budget – based on a ten-month, March-December fiscal year truncated to accommodate the shift of the fiscal year to January 1 as of 1983 – may have closed with a larger deficit than initially foreseen. The original 1982 budget called for expenditures of $9.4 million and revenues of $8.9 million, a short fall of $500 million. Recent tentative estimates indicate that expenditures may have risen somewhat less, to $8.3 million. Revenue receipts were also off the mark, attaining only $7.9 billion. If these data prove accurate, the budget deficit for fiscal 1982 was $500 million, which on a twelve-month basis corresponds to 1.2 percent of GNP (1.6 percent in 1981). While ratios may not seem excessive by international comparison, they should not be taken lightly as the public sector deficit must add to the financial strains in an economy where capital is scarce. In particular, public sector investments, notably in social and economic infrastructure, have had to be cut back in recent years for budgetary reasons. If the deficit cannot be held under control, public investments which are urgently needed to support economic growth will suffer further delays.

3.5 TAX REFORM. After several ill-fated attempts at tax reform in the late 1970s, a major tax reform program was enacted in late 1980; several additional measures have been promulgated subsequently. The reform program is designed to increase the immediate yield and insure the continued effectiveness of the tax system, and to remove the inequity arising from the payment of little or no tax by a large segment of the population.

There are six principal elements to the tax reform. First, income tax rates and exemptions applicable to wage earners have been restructured to correct inflationary distortions in the tax system. Second, the previously minor taxation of professionals and the self-employed has been increased by raising the lump-sum tax on small businessmen and instituting a new system of income tax payments for the self-employed. Such taxes are to be paid in advance in installments based on an assessed level of income determined by local commissions, with the assessment contestable only at the end of the tax year. Third, the earnings of farmers are being taxed for the first time on a systematic basis by means of a withholding tax on sales of agricultural products. Fourth, various fixed-rate indirect taxes and duties have been increased substantially. Fifth, the revenue base of the municipalities has been strengthened considerably, by raising revenues and by providing for five percent of government tax revenues to be withheld at the local level. Sixth, tax administration is being strengthened, new tax courts established, and heavier penalties imposed for tax evasion. In the future, the government wishes to implement a value-added tax.

Tax credits against income have been introduced tor certain exporters, and for contractors, tourist organizations, and other foreign exchange earners. The government realizes that the full revenue impact of the tax reform cannot be achieved until administrative arrangements have been strengthened.

4. PETROLEUM AND ENERGY SECTOR

4.1 GENERAL. Despite the potential of its natural resources, Turkey still faces an energy shortage. Turkey's production of petroleum is able to meet only about 15 percent of domestic consumption; the rest of the demand is met by imports. (Petroleum and its derivatives represent approximately 75 percent of Turkey's yearly imports.) Crude oil imports alone were 10.5 million tons in 1980, 11.6 million tons in 1981, and 13.5 million tons in 1982, for which Turkey paid $2.6, $3.3 and $3.4 billion, respectively. The phasing out, since 1980, of the large subsidies for petroleum and its products and the consequent sharp increases in domestic oil prices are expected to lead to a further shift in the consumption pattern away from petroleum to other forms of energy.

Geological studies and oil drillings carried out for more than 40 years have revealed that Turkey does not share the vast oil beds existing in neighboring countries. Nevertheless, there might be substantial deep-lying reserves. Since the exploration for rich but deep-lying reserves from as much as 15,000 to 45,000 feet requires considerable expense and highly sophisticated equipment, it will be difficult for Turkey to attain the desired level in the production of oil.

4.2 RECENT DEVELOPMENTS. The government encourages foreign participation in the exploration for and production of oil. The basic law regulating foreign participation in this sector was adopted in 1954 in an effort to promote the rapid, continuous and efficient development of Turkey's oil resources. Liberal fiscal regulations were established to encourage exploration and foreign participation, which have been amended periodically by succesive governments. In March 1983, a new and more liberal petroleum law was enacted which gives foreign companies greater incentives.

The first major discovery of oil in Turkey occurred in 1940 with the Raman field in the southeastern part of the country. In addition to The Turkish Petroleum Company (TPAO), both Shell and Mobil have been active in the past in all phases of exploration and development in Turkey. Production in 1981 totaled approximately 2.4 million metric tons, a slight increase over the 1980 level. Since exploration began in Turkey, 582 exploration wells have been drilled, with a success rate above the world average. Including extension, development and injection wells, a total of 1,765 wells have been drilled. However, Turkey remains largely unexplored and the government is hopeful that its new economic policies and investment incentives will increase exploration activities. To date, several foreign companies have either applied for exploration licenses or are negotiating joint venture agreements with TPAO.

4.3 ENERGY OUTLOOK. Other sources of energy available to Turkey include thermal fuel production from lignite and coal. Turkey's coal output totaled 7,181 metric tons in 1982, a slight decrease from 1981. Lignite production was more promising: 20,133 metric tons in 1982, a 6.5 percent increase from 1981.

Another source of energy with excellent potential is hydroelectric power from Turkey's many rivers. Total potential power generation from hydroelectric power is estimated at 100,000 KWH. However, even if fully exploited, hydroelectric power would not make Turkey self-sufficient in energy.

In 1982, Turkey produced 26,552 KWH of electricity, of which 12,383 was from thermal power, and 14,169 from hydroelectric power. This was not sufficient to meet total demand in 1982, estimated at approximately 29,000 KWH. Some 1,800 KWH had to be imported from Bulgaria and the Soviet Union. Power shortages and cuts were also experienced by electricity users.

5. INDUSTRY AND MINING

5.1 BACKGROUND. Development policies in modern Turkey traditionally favored import substitution over exports and industry over agriculture, with public enterprises playing an important role in the economy. After initial success, these policies encountered increasing difficulties as high-cost import substitution, aggravated by inefficiencies in public enterprises, led to a decline in the productivity of investment.

Since the 1930's Turkey has attempted to spur industrialization. The products of its heavy industry facilities, such as steel mills and aluminum plants, are not competitive on the world market. For some two decades, Turkey has had an assembly industry for automobiles and trucks, electronic goods, and other complex products, the basic parts for which are imported from the west. Light industry has been developing especially rapidly. The textile sector has performed strongly in recent years. Yet on the whole, Turkey still lacks a modernized industrial base which could allow it to meet European competition if present customs protection were removed.

Value added in industry, the growth of which had averaged 10 percent before the crisis, fell by about 2 percent per year during 1978-1980, and by almost 6 percent in 1980, as a result of bottlenecks arising from lack of imported inputs and a proliferation of strikes. With the return to better supply conditions and the end of industrial unrest, this process was reversed in 1981; value added increased by some 7 percent, although from a depressed level. The moderate rate of industrial growth in 1982 (3.2 percent) reflects more accurately the tight policy stance.

5.2 GROWTH PATTERNS Until 1977, high rates of economic growth were maintained by raising the share of investment in the gross domestic product. The rise in investment was financed by savings from worker remittances and, following the quadrupling of oil prices in 1973-1977, increasingly by foreign borrowing. Rising external indebtedness in turn raised questions concerning Turkey's credit-worthiness. As a result, foreign borrowing practically ceased in 1978, creating a foreign exhange scarcity that aggravated the adverse economic effects of the import-substitution policies.

The policy reforms introduced in January 1980 were aimed not only at redressing the economic situation, but also at changing the development strategy Turkey had followed for several decades. The newly-adopted strategy has entailed moving towards outward orientation (export promotion and increased import substitution) and giving an increased role to market forces.

Industrial production in Turkey increased by 7.2 percent in 1981 and about 3.2 percent in 1982, compared to a decline of 5.8 percent in 1980. This turnaround in industrial output was the result of an easing of the supply situation following the inflow of foreign exchange and an improvement in labor relations. Capacity utilization in the industrial sector, which has been low in recent years, rose significantly in 1982, and stood at 66.8 percent (compared to 62 percent in 1981 and 51 percent in 1980).

Industry accounted for 11.9 percent of employment in 1982, growing 1.6 percent from the previous year. It accounted for 27.7 percent of GDP in 1982.

5.3 MANUFACTURING. Total production in the manufacturing sector was $29.69 billion in 1981 (at 1982 prices). Production went up to $31.28 billion in 1982, a 5.4 percent increase. For 1983, manufactured production stood at $33.20 billion (at 1982 prices), an increase of 6.1 percent.

The composition of industry has shifted over the last twenty years. Investment goods have fluctuated in importance, but no clear trend can be detected. On the other hand, there is nothing equivocal about the increase in the share of the intermediate goods industry at the expense of consumer goods; by 1982, the share of the latter had dropped to 48.2 percent of industrial production from 62.3 percent in 1962, while that of intermediate goods had risen from 21.8 percent to 41.2 percent over the same period.

In 1982 the rate of increase in intermediate goods production was 9 percent, and 8 percent for investment goods. In 1981, these rates were 9.3 and 9 percent, respectively. This is a significant increase in the production of both intermediate and investment goods. On the other hand, the rate of increase in the production of consumer goods fell to 1.9 percent in 1982 from 7.7 percent in 1981. The main reasons for this drop were the decline in domestic demand, difficulties encountered in financing production, and the reduction of export opportunities in 1982 over 1981. However, in 1983 the estimated increase in the production of consumer goods was 5.2 percent.

Despite the drops recorded in the volume of world trade in 1982 and increasing protectionist tendencies pursued by industrialized countries, Turkey's export of industrial products has increased 49.7 percent over the previous year. The share of industrial products in Turkish exports rose to 59.7 percent in 1982, from a 49.7 percent level in 1981.

These favorable developments were the results of the new economic policies:

- Implementation of a more realistic and flexible currency rate policy.
- Granting to exporting industrialists the right of duty-free importation of inputs of raw materials and intermediate goods.
- The selective credit system and tax rebates for exports.

5.4 **MINING.** Turkey has most of the natural resources to support rapid economic development. It has coal to supply its three steel mills, but lacks enough high-grade iron ore for their efficient operation. While low-grade coal and lignite is produced in quantities that meet domestic needs, Turkey's main energy deficiency is in oil; about eighty percent of the petroleum needed must be imported.

Turkey has a good supply of most other minerals; in particular, it is a major source of chrome. The new Turkish economic program applied since January 1980 explicitly recognized the waste of resources resulting from past policies and has attempted to correct those mistakes. In an attempt to develop Turkey's extensive mineral resource base more rapidly, the government reopened the mining sector to foreign investment in January 1980. This decision represented a marked departure from policies pursued in the past. Presently, except for coal, lignite and certain strategic minerals which were nationalized, foreign mining companies are being encouraged to engage in exploration and development activities for all minerals in Turkey.

Although various investment arrangements are acceptable, the government's preference is for tripartite joint ventures comprising Etibank (a SEE and the principal state-owned mining corporation), the Turkish private mining sector, and foreign partners. This particular arrangement offers the advantage of opening up to private investment some of the better known and larger mineral deposits for which Etibank presently holds both exploration and operating licenses. As regards legislation, the government is in the process of redrafting the current Turkish mining law.

To date, several large international mining companies have shown an interest in certain projects which Etibank has selected for joint development. These comprise projects for copper, aluminum, marble, pumice, perlite, and volcanic tuffs. Interest is also being shown in minerals such as chromite, barite and bentonite.

6. AGRICULTURAL SECTOR

6.1 GENERAL. Although the inward-oriented development strategy followed by Turkey discriminated against agriculture in favor of industry, agricultural production is still very important for the country's development. The Country's land and labor resources, favorable climate, and proximity to expanding markets will permit a rapid increase in agricultural production and exports in the near future, provided that appropriate policies are followed.

To exploit its climatic advantage, Turkey has in the past decade substantially increased its production of early spring market vegetables in addition to making steady gains in the production of wheat and other traditional products such as hazel nuts, tobacco and dried fruits. Export of these products makes a significant contribution to Turkey's foreign exchange earnings. Cotton, produced in irrigated fields in the Aegean and Adana regions, supplies an expanding textile industry. Although agricultural productivity is rising with the introduction of higher yielding varieties and improved breeds as well as with the increased use of fertilizer and insecticides, Turkish agriculture is still relatively inefficient in comparison with European farming.

Turkey's agriculture has the potential to produce a rich array of continental products (i.e., cereals, cotton, tobacco and livestock) and Mediterranean crops (fruits and vegetables). This fact reflects the variety of soils and agroclimatic zones in the country, and the threefold role of agriculture as (i) domestic supplier of final consumption goods, (ii) domestic supplier of raw materials for industrial transformation, and (iii) foreign exchange earner.

6.2 SPECIALIZATION. Despite the variety of its agroclimatic conditions, Turkey's agricultural sector is greatly specialized. In 1980, 71 percent of the cultivated area was devoted to cereals, of which wheat and barley accounted for 85 percent. None of the other crops account for a substantial part of the total cultivated area. Sugar beets, oil seeds, cotton, and tobacco account for 9 percent of the cultivated area, olives and grapes for 8 percent, fruits and nuts for 7 percent, vegetables for 4 percent, pulses for 3 percent, and tea for 1 percent.

Turkey has, in addition, 21 million hectares of natural pastures, which support one of the largest animal populations in Europe and the Middle East. This includes 64 million sheep and goats, 16 million cattle and buffalo, 2.5 million horses, donkeys and mules, and 55 million poultry.

6.3 PRODUCTS. Agricultural products in Turkey may be classified into four categories:

- Import substitution crops: wheat, sugar beets, sunflower seeds, and tea. These products have received considerable encouragement in the last twenty years in the form of price supports, the allocation of subsidized inputs, and the provision of the extension services, the aim being to increase self-sufficiency.
- Traditional export crops: nuts, dried fruits, and tobacco. Turkish export of these products constituted a sizeable share in world trade, with 70 percent for hazelnuts, about 25 percent for dry figs, 20 percent for raisins, and 20 percent for oriental tobacco.
- Major export crops: cotton, pulses, roots and olive oil. This group includes staple exports which are widely traded on the world market.
- Fruits and vegetables, including root crops (potatoes and onions); and livestock and livestock products.

6.4 OUTPUT. Import substitution crops registered the largest increase in terms of cultivated area, production and yield over the 1960-79 period.

Production increases in traditional crops were modest, with the exception of hazelnuts, whose production rose by more than 100 percent. The yields from olive trees decreased by about 10 percent.

Over the same period, citrus fruit production increased by over 200 percent and vegetable production by some 50 percent. Since the domestic prices of fruits and vegetables are not supported, and government intervention in their production is minimal, the substantial increase in production and in product-specialization within the sector must be attributed to market forces.

The number of sheep and goats increased by only 10 percent during the 1960-79 period, while cattle and buffalo increased by 22 percent. As a result, the production of sheep and goat products stagnated whereas meat and milk from cattle and buffalo increased by 82 percent and 17 percent respectively. In the poultry sector a remarkable increase in the number of hens occurred, leading to a rise in egg production of over 200 percent.

According to official estimates, value added in agriculture virtually stagnated in 1981, but recovered briskly in 1982. This fluctuation is to some extent due to a statistical bias – official estimates probably underestimated the rise in value added in 1981, particularly in respect to wheat production. Even so, agricultural output was negatively affected in 1981 by disappointing yields of some major crops, mainly due to reduced application of fertilizers, the trough of the bi-annual olive production cycle, and a change in the government purchasing policy on tea and tobacco aimed at reducing overproduction and improving quality.

By contrast, the recovery in 1982 can be explained by the increased use of fertilizers, whose prices were not raised in the course of the year, the peak of the olive production cycle, increases in tea and tobacco production of presumably better quality, and rises in livestock production.

6.5 INFRASTRUCTURE. Considerable infrastructural investments in the 1970s have reduced the dependence of agriculture on climate conditions. At the present time, agriculture accounts for 20 percent of GDP and about 60 percent of employment. However, agricultural output on average is not growing much faster than the population. This constitutes an obvious constraint on the expansion of agricultural exports, which could be overcome by the improvement in yields for which there appears to be large potential.

In the future, the government expects that the market-oriented measures it has adopted will stimulate productivity per hectare which will allow Turkey to increase its production and export of grain, fruit, vegetables and livestock.

Agriculture accounted for 61 percent of employment in 1982, employment in agriculture having declined 0.3

percent from the previous year. It accounted for 20.7 percent of GDP in 1982, a decline from the 1977 level of 27.6 percent.

7. MANPOWER

7.1 DOMESTIC EMPLOYMENT CONDITIONS. Estimates of the population of Turkey stand at a figure in excess of 46 million. Because the participation rate (63.5 percent) is fairly high despite the high proportion of young people in the population and the relatively limited opportunities for women, Turkey has a large economically-active population: roughly 15.5 million. This circumstance is one of the major determinants of the nature of the Turkish economy; unlike a number of Middle Eastern states that have severe labor shortages, Turkey has a labor surplus.

Agriculture is by far the largest employer. An estimated 9,481,000 people (or 61.3 percent of the population employed in civilian occupations) are employed in agriculture. Of these, about 7 percent, or 665,000 are believed to be victims of disguised unemployment; in other words, while they earn a living of sorts in agriculture, the marginal productivity of their labor is negligible (in view of the saturation of the agricultural sector), and their wages, in consequence, tend to be barely sufficient for subsistence. This pattern is not uncommon in developing countries where a low level of industrialization results in an "uncommercialized" agricultural sector, with attendant underutilization of manpower.

The portion of the population engaged in manufacturing is approximately 10.5 percent of the total (1982 estimates). Productivity in the industrial sector is significantly higher than in the agricultural; in 1982, value added per laborer in agriculture was estimated to be fully 85.4 percent lower than in industry. The huge discrepancy in productivity has accounted for the growth of the manufacturing sector at the expense of agriculture; the percentage of GDP (at current prices) accounted for by agriculture fell from 39.4 in 1962 to 20.7 percent in 1982, while the percentage accounted for by industry has grown from 16.1 percent to 27.7 percent over the corresponding period. Meanwhile, labor has shifted away from agriculture, lured by the higher wages.

The "service sector," broadly defined to include construction, accounts for a miniscule proportion of civilian employment. However, labor productivity in the sector is nearly as high as in industry, and accounts for over half (51.6 percent) of GDP at current prices. This has created an uncomfortable situation for manpower development. The capacity of the service sector to generate employment is limited; what employment it offers is highly cyclical and greatly responsive to the overall level of economic activity. Yet, in terms of value added, the sector continues to dominate the economy; its continued prosperity can be attributed to the fact that, unlike manufacturing (which is the only realistic hope for generating enough adequately rewarding employment), it has minimal investment requirement.

7.2 UNEMPLOYMENT AND UNDEREMPLOYMENT. In addition to the imbalance in manpower development, Turkey is plagued with a high unemployment and underemployment rate. Political instability, coupled with labor unrest, contributed to low growth and consequent limited job opportunities, especially for young people. In 1982, an estimated 14.5 percent of the economically active population was unemployed – and this without taking into account disguised unemployment in agriculture. The deteriorating situation is illustrated by the fact that the unemployment rate grew an average 11.3 percent during the period 1978-82.

If disguised unemployment in agriculture is taken into account, the total estimate for the unemployment rate rises to 18.2 percent, having increased an average 15.4 percent over the period 1978-82. This does not take into account the 2.2 million people estimated to be in the non-agricultural surplus labor category, although it should be noted that that estimate is highly speculative.

The high unemployment and underemployment, which would normally have occasioned enormous social dislocation, has had less serious effects in Turkey than might be expected. This is due to:

- The extended family system, which (in the absence of a comprehensive social security system) provides a network of support for the unemployed and those barely able to subsist. It also mitigates the odium associated with the necessity to accept low-paying jobs.
- The preoccupation with political stability, which superseded economic worries for some time,

particularly when it erupted into violence in the late 1970's.
- Emigration has lessened the pressure on the domestic economy, making it possible for many to find employment abroad while continuing to provide for relatives at home.
- The government sector has acted as an employer of the last resort to many who could not find work elsewhere, absorbing in particular university graduates who fail to find jobs, even at the risk of increasing bureaucratic inefficiency. Since the initiation of the stabilization program, however, public sector employment, including the State Economic Enterprises, has remained constant at approximately two million people.

The military junta which took over in 1980 assigned a high priority to restoring political and social stability, temporarily relegating the economy to second place. At the same time, the "pacification process" entailed breaking the power of the unions, which, coupled with low growth, resulted in the continued growth of unemployment (from 11.4 in 1980 to 14.5 in 1982). The new Ozal cabinet, which took power in 1983, while beholden to the military to a large extent, has chosen to focus on economic problems - low growth and unemployment being the most severe of these. While the government has scored some success in maintaining economic growth in the face of worldwide recession, its concern about curbing inflation suggests that its commitment to lowering unemployment is less than total.

7.3 LABOR MIGRATION. Emigration has been a safety mechanism allowing the economy to continue to function while a large number of people are unable to find work domestically. In 1982, estimates of Turks working abroad varied betwen 979,000 and 1,064,000. More than half of these are working in Germany as "Gastarbeiter," meaning that they are employed for a limited period without being considered immigrants, and so eventually must return home.

The slowdown of economic activity in Germany and other European countries where Turks are employed has resulted in serious difficulties, with opportunities drying up and forced repatriation becoming a common occurrence. Meanwhile, those Turks remaining in Europe encounter problems, in particular racial prejudice, cultural disorientation for themselves and their children, and various forms of discrimination. Furthermore, the reliance on emigration to mitigate unemployment may have resulted in distorted priorities in the minds of Turkish planners (with other problems receiving attention while unemployment is neglected), in greater Turkish dependence on the EEC, and in greater sensitivity to cyclical movements in foreign economies.

An interesting phenomenon of late is the exportation of workers to other Middle Eastern states. Libya was at one time an attractive destination for Turkish workers, but economic difficulties there suggest that not many more Turkish workers can find employment in that market. Saudi Arabia, where an estimated 80,000 Turkish workers are now employed, has tacitly indicated a preference for Turkish workers in certain sectors, notably construction. Turkish workers offer the Saudis the advantage of cultural compatibility (because of their religion) with minimal potential for agitation (because of the language barrier).

7.4 LABOR UNIONS The most activist large union, the confederation of Progressive Trade Unions (known by its Turkish initials as "DISK") was effectively suppressed in 1980 as a direct consequence of the military coup. The pro-government Turkish Trade Unions Confederation (Turk-Is) is permitted to operate, although it seems to command little loyalty among workers; likewise it offers limited appeal to left-leaning intellectuals, who are quick to point out its ties to the American Federation of Labor and other distinctly non-socialist unions world-wide.

A major part of the disorder which gave the impetus to the 1980 military coup was the high incidence of strike activities, which debilitated the economy and eroded business confidence. In 1980, there were no less than 220 strikes (a record), with a total of 84,832 participants (another record), resulting in yet another record total of work days lost: 7,708,750, nearly seven times the number of days lost in 1979.

The military government was ruthless in suppressing independent union activity as an attempt both to curb a potential focus for opposition and to re-order society in a fashion the junta regarded as compatible with its concept of economic justice and with Turkey's best interests. In practice, the latter objective has meant the imposition of stringent regulations on unionization and strikes, mainly in the form of Law 2821 on Trade Unions, Collective Bargaining, Strikes and Lock-outs, passed in May 1983. The law makes it difficult for unions (other than the docile Turk-Is) to be constituted, makes joining a union a complicated and risky process for a worker, and imposes strict limitations on strikes.

The resulting shift of the balance against the working class has greatly reduced the incidence of labor unrest, and caused average net wages to grow so slowly relative to inflation that they declined in real terms in the immediate aftermath of the coup. While this has helped restore business confidence, the cost in terms of alienation of workers should not be underestimated.

The civilian government which took power in late 1983 is closely associated with the middle class: entrepreneurs, salaried civil servants, farmers, rather than factory workers. As such, a relaxation of restrictions on union activities is not likely. Many regard this situation as tenable for some time because it conforms to the "Kemalist" model of paternalistic government "interest" in labor problems in a supposedly "classless" (but actually corporativist) setting. However, the fact that labor disaffection has intensified rather than abated points to a potentially explosive situation.

8. CONSTRUCTION AND HOUSING

8.1 GENERAL. The construction and housing sector has been one of the fields which has suffered most from economic recession since 1978. Since the economic stability measures of 1980, a vitality has been observed in most branches of industry. However, the recession in the construction and housing sector still continues.

The increase in total value added of the construction sector in 1968 prices has been 0.8 percent in 1980, 0.4 percent in 1981, and 0.5 percent in 1982.

The main reason for this recession seems to be the ever-increasing rate of construction costs, overall economic stagnation worldwide, a mood of fiscal austerity, and saturation in some project areas.

Both public and private sectors are active in construction and housing. The investments of the public sector are oriented mainly to meeting the need for basic infrastructure, while the private sector is active in the construction of business buildings and housing.

Public investment in construction has shown a remarkable decrease since 1977. In 1977, 35 percent of Turkey's total budget was appropriated for construction projects. This ratio has dropped to 20 percent in recent years. The investments of the private sector are also decreasing. Fixed capital investments by the private sector dropped, in real terms, from $1.7 billion in 1978 to $1.1 billion in 1982. Private investment in housing was a mere 2.09 percent of GNP in 1982, and was estimated to be 2.11 percent of GNP in 1983.

Statistics on construction starts and building permits issued have shown a discouraging trend since 1977. The recession in the construction and housing affects the related sub-branches of the industry adversely and reduces the employment opportunities that this sector used to offer on a large scale. Furthermore, with the 2.2 percent increase in population, the actual need for housing continued to be an important social issue, adding to the urgent "basic needs gap" of the country.

8.2 POLICIES. Despite increasing concern in recent years, this sector failed to attain the desired level of activity. Some measures were envisaged in the 1983 program for the purpose of reactivating the construction sector:

- A higher priority is accorded in the public sector to infrastructure projects.
- Time-consuming bureaucratic formalities have been reduced, especially in connection with public sector construction.
- Appropriation of funds to "organized industrial zones" and "light industry facilities" has been increased.
- Housing legislation concerning the construction of public housing projects and the mobilization of individual savings is in the process of revision.
- A set of incentives are envisaged for self-help housing activity in the form of low interest rates. Subsidized public loans are promised for firms engaged in constructing and selling low-cost buildings.
- A gradual tax reduction is envisaged in the construction sector; where taxes presently constitute 30 percent of the overall expenditures.

8.3 CONSTRUCTION AND THE FOREIGN SECTOR. Turkish construction firms have succeeded in establishing an international presence, particularly in oil-rich Middle Eastern states, where they have the advantage of geographic proximity, familiarity with the terrain and business practices, a history of good relations, reasonable labor costs, and a relatively good reputation for labor docility.

Three Turkish construction firms are among the 100 largest in the world. These are: Enka Insaat & Sanayi, Kutlutas, and Libas. In 1982, Turkish firms had 3.7 percent of the Middle Eastern market and 2.2 percent of the world market.

Turkey's major construction clients in the Middle East are Libya, Saudi Arabia, and Iraq. Iraq and Iran offer the possibility of a larger role for Turkish firms once the Gulf War is concluded, as the reconstruction effort will require massive foreign participation.

9. FINANCIAL SECTOR

9.1 CENTRAL BANK. The major components of the banking and financial system in Turkey are the Central Bank of the Republic of Turkey (the "Central Bank"), the deposit money banks, the investment and development banks and, to a limited but growing extent, the domestic capital market. As a consequence of government market-oriented policies taken to redress the economic and financial difficulties of the late 1970s, the banking and financial system in Turkey is being subjected to operational change and increased competition.

The basic duties of the Central Bank are to administer money and credit policies in conformity with development plans and annual programs to manage the government's foreign exchange dealings, to regulate the volume and circulation of the currency, to refinance bank lending, and to hold the official international reserves of the country. Since May 1, 1981, the Central Bank has been given the authority to adjust daily the rates of exchange of the Turkish lira against all traded currencies. In general, the Central Bank performs the duties of economic advisor, financial agent, and treasurer with regard to the government; the government consults the Central Bank as necessary when taking measures concerning money and credit.

In January 1980 the goverment established a Money and Credit Council to coordinate all of its monetary and financial policy decisions. The Council consists of the Deputy Prime Minister, who is chairman, and senior representatives of the Ministry of Finance, the Ministry of Commerce, the State Planning Organization, and the Central Bank. Once a decision has been taken by the Council, the relevant authorities in Turkey are requested to take the necessary steps toward implementation.

9.2 BANKING SYSTEM. The banking system in Turkey consists of forty five banks including the Central Bank. Of these, twenty six are indigenous, privately-owned institutions, and five are foreign-owned. The major commercial banks are internationally known institutions with nationwide branch networks and deposit bases. Some thirty two commercial banks and one investment and development bank are authorized to deal in foreign exchange. Such banks, which presently enjoy increasing autonomy in their foreign exchange transactions, are permitted to retain 80 percent of their foreign exchange proceeds, up to a limit of $25 million. The main function of the five investment and development banks, of which two are publicly-owned, is to provide medium- and long-term credit to industrial companies in both the private and public sectors.

Prior to January 1980, four foreign banks were operating in Turkey, some with branch systems: the Ottoman Bank, Banco di Roma, Arab-Turkish Bank, and Hollandische Bank-Unie. Since January 1980, foreign banks have been encouraged to open branches throughout Turkey and generally permitted to operate with the same rights as indigenous banks. By the end of 1981, four foreign commercial banks had been granted authorization to open full-fledged branch operations in Turkey: American Express International Banking Corporation, Bank of Credit and Commerce International, Bank Mellat, and Citibank. Under the regulations which apply to the opening of branches by foreign banks, promulgated in October 1981, a foreign bank is permitted to open no more than five branches in Turkey. The first branch is required to have capital of $6 million, subsequent branches must have capital of $3 million. In addition, one Turkish bank operates a branch in Germany and others have established operations in New York, London, and Bahrain. Publicly-owned banks have 40.9 percent of all bank branches in Turkey; privately-owned banks have 57.1 percent; foreign banks have 2.0 percent.

Banks in Turkey are controlled and supervised by the Ministry of Finance and the Central Bank. The main purpose of regulation is to protect deposits and provide monetary control; another aim is to allocate credit on the basis of planning priorities. All banks are subject to limitations on the rates of interest paid on sight deposits, but are free to establish rates of interest on time deposits and on loans. With respect to commercial banks, the government and the Central Bank control rediscounts, determine reserve deposit and liquidity requirements, set the rates of guarantee and advance deposits for imports, and regulate their external positions. In April 1981 the Central Bank introduced a new export credit system which simplifies export administrative procedures including all phases of export financing under the rediscount system.

Credit. Lending by the Central Bank, which is directed to the Treasury, public enterprises, deposit money banks, and investment and development banks, has generally been allocated on policy grounds through the use of commercial rediscounts and preferential credits. Deposit money banks, the traditional lenders to the private sector, increased their lending activities significantly in 1980 and 1981. Total bank lending was fairly evenly divided between the public and private sectors until 1980, when lending to the private sector grew by an increasing margin, reflecting the improvement in public finances. During the transition to a market-oriented financial system, lending by the banking system will continue to be sector-oriented for the near future. Non-specialized financial intermediaries and inter-bank lending are not fully developed at present.

Two important banking developments took place in mid-1983. The first deals with the interest rates. Effective July 1, 1983, interest rates on one-year deposits were reduced from 45 percent to 40 percent, and the rates on six-month savings from 40 to 35 percent. Sight deposits remained at 20 percent, commercial deposits remained non-interest-bearing.

Commercial credit rates became 32 percent instead of 36 percent, and the rates on export loans were reduced to 26.5 percent from the previous level of 31.5 percent. On medium-term industrial loans over two years, the rates are 34 percent instead of 38 percent.

While export-guaranteed investment credits to be used in the financing of projects in the development of high-priority regions are 19 percent, investment loans secured for the shipping industry are 23 percent.

New Bank Law. Another development is the long-awaited new Bank Law. The new law contains many important principles, requirements and rules, including:

- The banks will be expected to have a minimum of 100 partners to function as a joint stock company.
- Each bank will be required to have one billion TL ($2.8 million) private capital in order to be established.
- Savings deposit accounts of up to three billion TL ($8.4 million) will be insured. For this scheme, an insurance fund will be established and monitored by the Central Bank.
- No bank will be permitted to give credit loans totaling more than 10 percent of its own capital.

- Time deposits will be for a minimum of six months.
- The administrative boards of banks will not consist of less than five people.

Banks have been reticent to support some of Ozal's liberalization measures. His lifting of exchange rate controls has caused banks to be saddled with enormous demand for foreign exchange which they must now take the time and trouble to satisfy. They have smarted at restrictive monetary measures that increase their already high borrowing costs. The introduction by the government of monthly interest rates to boost savings by small savers has drawn a skeptical response from the banking sector. The fact that no less than five banks have collapsed under severe pressure in the past year (the last being the small Bagbank) has caused banks to be nervous; even the reduction of the bank transaction tax from 15 to 3 percent has failed to boost confidence.

9.3 CAPITAL MARKET. The capital market in Turkey is presently of limited importance. Its development is being stimulated both by direct government action and by result of the government's market-oriented economic policies. Government securities have comprised the principal element of the domestic capital market, but, until recently, issuance has been limited due to direct government borrowing from the Central Bank to finance its borrowing requirements. In 1982, local bond issues totalled $1.54 billion, of which 85 percent was for public sector bonds. Private sector shares worth $0.58 billion were also issued in 1982.

9.4 MONEY AND CREDIT. As one of the key elements in its effort to reduce the rate of inflation, the government is determined to maintain strict control of the rate of monetary expansion. Stabilization policies in 1978 and 1979 were not able to sustain meaningful overall monetary improvements, but measures implemented in the 1980 economic program, which are still in effect, are resulting in overall improvements in the monetary sector.

The main policy objectives of the government are to limit domestic demand, control the growth of the money supply, mobilize domestic savings, improve resource allocation, and encourage exports by channeling credit to the export sector. To realize these objectives, the government is pursuing measures which include the following: strict observance of a tight monetary policy, discipline with respect to public finances, maintenance of a liberalized bank lending and deposit interest rate policy in which rates are determined by market forces, and promotion of new instruments aimed at further mobilizing domestic savings.

In 1981, the money supply increased by 36.7 percent. This relatively low rate of monetary expansion has had a dampening effect on both the rate of inflation and the level of domestic demand. Industries oriented toward the domestic market, such as automobiles and consumer durables, have been adversely affected. Private fixed investment, except in export-oriented industries such as packaging, food, and transportation, also suffered from the low level of domestic demand.

Liquidity. The main reason for increases in overall liquidity in the late 1970s was the continued increase in Central Bank credits, particularly to fund deficits in the public sector. Total credits of the Central Bank increased by 71.5 percent in 1980, when 63.0 percent of those credits went directly to the public sector. However, in 1980, for the first time in recent years, Central Bank credits to the private sector grew faster than those to the public sector. This trend continued in 1981, while the share of Central Bank credit to the public sector continued to decline. In 1980, the increase in total Central Bank credits was reduced to 41.3 percent; the increase in Central Bank credits to the public sector remained 31.1 percent and to the private sector, 58.6 percent.

The government's decision in July 1980 to free deposit interest rates had a significant effect on the growth of bank deposits even though a "gentleman's agreement" between a number of banks initially set uniform limits. For 1980, total deposits in deposit money banks increased 72.4 percent, time deposits increased 109.9 percent, evidencing a shift from sight to time deposits. Increased growth in deposits, most notably time deposits, was particularly marked in the second half of 1980. This trend accelerated in 1981; total deposits increased by 103.9 percent, with time deposits growing by 263.2 percent, and sight deposits by 50.7 percent. Throughout 1981, the minimum time deposit period was three months; since the beginning of 1982, time deposits of one- and two-month maturities have been offered.

Following the freeing of deposit interest rates in July 1980, lending rates rose significantly. General rates on short-term credits increased from 21 percent to 31 percent per annum, while general rates on medium-term credits rose from 22 percent to 33 percent and on long-term credits, from 22 percent to 36 percent. By the beginning of 1981, these rates had risen to 36 percent, 38 percent and 41 percent per annum, respectively. The combination of banks' differing competitive access to deposit funds and consequent borrowing costs, and their differing ability to assess lending risks, led to a breakdown in mid-1981 of the "gentleman's agreement" which had determined deposit rates. However, lending rates remained unchanged.

Tight Money. In the course of 1982, the tight monetary stance was modified to some extent by seasonal factors (the financing of the harvest), and by the need to provide liquidity support to a number of banks which were directly affected by the collapse of the broker "Banker Kastelli" in June. As a result, the year-to-year growth in money supply in the narrow definition (MI – money in circulation, commercial and sight savings deposits with the Central Bank), which had declined steadily from a peak of 61 percent in September 1980, to 23 percent in June 1982, rose considerably faster in the second half of the year, accelerating to 41 percent in December.

In 1982, three factors created difficulties in restricting the growth of money supply in line with the intitial inflation target. First, the contribution of net foreign assets became positive as of the last quarter of 1981. Second, the large wheat harvest in the summer meant an increase in support purchases by state agencies. Third, the collapse of Banker Kastelli made an injection of additional liquidity into the banking system necessary. This could only partly be compensated for by restrictions on credit expansion. Thus, Central Bank credit to the public sector increased by only 5 percent and credits to the private sector – adjusted for debt rescheduling – rose by no more than 4 percent. Taking inflation into account, there has been a considerable reduction in real terms (by about 20 percent) in Central Bank credits to the economy.

Commercial Lending. Commercial bank lending has slowed under the influence of the tightening of Central Bank credit, as well as through lack of demand due to high real rates of interest. While total credits by commercial banks (excluding investment banks) had increased by 67 percent in 1981, they rose by only 28 percent in 1982. Investment bank credit rose by 18 percent, compared to 45 percent a year earlier. To some extent, commercial banks were also affected adversely by the Kastelli crash and by the liquidity problems of private sector enterprises which experienced difficulties in adjusting to the new economic policy environment. Some commercial bank credits appear to have become non-performing, but banks have been affected unevenly, with some in a worse situation than others.

The government acted quickly to prevent a panic in June 1982 by guaranteeing payment of normal interest and principal on deposit certificates and bonds surrendered as security against deposits by the brokers, and by allowing banks in temporary trouble to call on emergency funding from the Central Bank. Savers reacted by shifting funds from the smaller banking institutions to larger banks, notably those owned or backed by the State. The larger banks found the increase in deposits a mixed blessing because of the prevailing high real interest rates paid and the difficulties in finding enough first-class borrowers in a recessionary environment. Moreover, with profits declining and the proportion of doubtful loans increasing, commercial banks are beginning to feel the consequences of an outdated organizational structure. The majority of Turkish banks have an over-extended branch network and lack modern business organization, entailing high overhead costs. Turkish banking has been characterized by low capitalization, which makes banks more vulnerable in a crisis. Traditional links with the State or large private business interests strongly influence the composition of loan portfolios.

The continued monetary expansion has caused the inflation rate to remain high. In 1982 and 1983 it stood at approximately 40 percent. The Ozal government has announced its intention to cut inflation to 25 percent, but most experts regard this goal as unrealistic. They expect inflation to remain around 40 percent, and possibly to increase if economic recovery begins in earnest.

9.5 COST OF CREDIT. Several measures designed to lower the cost of credit were introduced at the beginning of 1983. Interest rates on time deposits (6-12 months) were lowered by ten points to 40 percent, and by five points to 45 percent on one-year deposits which, with inflation increasing by only about 25 percent, amounts to real gross interest rates between 15 and 20 percent. In order to make time deposits somewhat less attractive and provide better inflation-proofing of ordinary savings accounts, the interest rate on sight savings deposits was raised from 5 percent to 20 percent. The withholding tax on interest earnings was generally set at 20 percent, and the fiscal balance tax on incomes was abolished.

Steps were taken to reduce operating costs of banks. The liquidity ratio of banks was lowered from a maximum 15 percent of deposits to a flat 10 percent, while the category of assets taken into account in calculating it was extended. Reserve requirements at the Central Bank, which were 35 and 30 percent for sight and time deposits respectively (but could be lower depending on the type of preferential loan business banks accepted), were unified at 25 percent. Central Bank interest payments on reserves have been raised. These measures are expected to lower costs for banks by 5 to 7 percentage points. The banking transaction tax on credits, which is at present 15 percent, may also be reduced.

Profit Margin. The recent lowering of charges supported by the commercial banks, as well as the reduction of interest rates for time deposits, will improve the profit margin of banks. It could open the way to reducing the cost of credit, but the latter clearly still has a depressing influence on economic activity and discourages productive investment. Allowing for inflation, real interest rates for deposits are now in the region of 15 percent, while for ordinary loans they are higher, owing partly to bank commissions. However, these rates were instrumental in attracting more savings and stopping the flight of money into real assets or bank accounts abroad. The composition of rates available to financial investors needs to be managed judiciously in order to arrive at a sound structure, reflecting maturities and risks. This, in effect, means managing capital markets, particularly important at a time when many companies wish to increase borrowing and issue new shares. This is the implied aim of the new legislation to revalue companies' assets.

Simplified Regulations. The measures taken by the Turkish authorities so far, or contemplated for the near future, are clearly a step to simplify the maze of regulations surrounding banking operations and improve the performance of the money and capital market, both in a technical and substantive sense. The manner in which the beginning of a financial crisis in the summer of 1982 was handled deserves credit. The action was prompt, efficient and, apparently, equitable. It is essential to address problems of individual banks or enterprises in the same spirit and carry through the necessary reorganization for the long-term good of the economy.

10.
FOREIGN TRADE AND BALANCE OF PAYMENTS

10.1 GENERAL. The strong growth of domestic demand, the fall in the terms of trade following the first oil shock, and an overvalued currency were the major factors that led to current account deficits in the mid-1970s. In 1977 the current account deficit peaked at $3.4 billion or 7 percent of GNP. Following improvement in 1978 and 1979, owing to the introduction of a stabilization program and rescheduling of Turkey's foreign debt, the current deficit rose to $3.2 billion in 1980, mainly because of a doubling (in dollar terms) of the oil bill. The difficult balance-of-paymments position led to further debt rescheduling and financial aid from OECD governments, the World Bank, and the IMF.

Since mid-1980, however, the current account deficit has narrowed steadily to $1.091 billion in 1982 (or 2 percent of GNP), the smallest since 1974. The improvement was mainly attributable to the doubling of the value of exports (in dollars) between 1980 and 1982 – from $2.9 billion to $5.7 billion – which corresponded to a doubling of their share in GNP (from 5 to 11 percent). Special factors, such as export opportunities linked with events in the Middle East, partly explain this trend, but the decisive element seems to have been the new economic policy implemented since 1980, which has eliminated anti-export bias.

The trade balance (which, unlike the current account, excludes invisibles) continued to register a deficit in 1983. Indeed, the deficit for that year was estimated at $3.507 billion, 13.3 percent higher than the 1982 deficit, indicating that the military government had difficulties in boosting exports and controlling imports as it purported to do.

10.2 EXCHANGE RATE. Adjustment of the overvalued exchange rate to a more realistic level has been the main thrust of policy. The authorities sought to improve export competitiveness by depreciating the lira against foreign currencies. The dollar/lira exchange rate was depreciated by 23 percent in March 1978 and 44 percent in June 1979. However, because of the lack of effective control of inflation, these attempts were doomed to failure. The situation changed with the new economic policy at the beginning of 1980. Following a further 33 percent depreciation of the lira against the dollar in January, the authorities adopted a more flexible policy attitude to exchange rate management. Periodic small adjustments were made to the exchange rate, and beginning in June 1981, the rate has been adjusted daily. Furthermore, the complex system of multiple rates which had given a strong incentive to parallel foreign exchange markets was phased out by mid-1981.

As a result of this more flexible exchange rate management, and of the income and monetary policies implemented in 1980 which sharply decreased the rate of inflation, the real effective exchange rate did not show any upward trend between January 1980 and mid-1981; it fell by about 20 percent between then and the end of 1982. At the same time, these policies contributed to reducing the growth of domestic demand, releasing resources for exports. The profitability of exports relative to domestic sales was boosted by preferential access to subsidized credit, the remission of import taxes, tax rebates for export production, and the permission granted to exporters to use half of their foreign exchange earnings for future import requirements.

In late December, 1983, Ozal's civilian government took the unprecedented step of lifting foreign exchange control, allowing the lira to float freely for the first time in modern Turkish history. The result has been a sharp decline in the value of the lira, followed by an encouraging increase in export values in the first quarter of 1984 (36.5 percent over the first quarter of 1983). The purpose of the lifting of foreign exchange control was to "open" the economy and permit market forces to operate freely. While the long-term consequences of this step cannot be determined at this point, one definite result has been enhanced confidence in Turkey's economy on the part of the IMF and the international financial community, as evidenced by the government's success in raising a $300 million balance of payment support loan from a consortium of European banks in March, 1984, and in obtaining an IMF stand-by credit extension of SDR 250 million ($465 million) in January, 1984.

10.3 EXPORTS. Exports in dollar terms increased by 62 percent in 1981, with volume growth tentatively estimated at about 69 percent. Volume growth was still very buoyant in 1982 (34 percent), but sharply declining agricultural prices adversely affected export earnings, which increased by 22 percent in dollar value. The rapid growth of exports, especially in 1981, is explained by their initial low level as well as quick adjustment to new trading opportunities. The rise may to some extent be fictitious, reflecting statistical distortions. In the late 1970s, an overvalued lira, multiple exchange rates that discriminated against agricultural exports, and a flourishing parallel market for foreign exchange probably led to unrecorded exports of some traditional goods (e.g., livestock) and underinvoicing. These practices were reduced when the multiple exchange rates were phased out; exporters were allowed to hold part of their earnings in foreign currency, boosting customs data accordingly.

Export of processed and manufactured goods rose particularly rapidly in dollar terms – 120 percent in 1981 and 50 percent in 1982. This process has been characterized by the rapid growth of exports of products which had formerly accounted for a relatively low share of foreign sales, such as chemicals, rubber and plastic, petroleum products, iron and steel, metal products and machinery, electrical equipment, and motor vehicles. This has resulted in a diversification of manufactured exports: the share of textiles, clothing and leather in exports of manufactured goods, which had averaged about 60 percent between 1973 and 1979, fell to 37 percent in 1982. On the other hand, during the last two years, exports of agricultural goods (though not those of processed agricultural products) have been adversely affected by strong decreases in prices which have tended to offset large increases in volume. This was particularly the case during 1982, when dollar earnings fell by nearly 4 percent. Hence, the share of agricultural exports has fallen from 59 percent in 1979 to 37 percent in 1982.

In 1981 and 1982, there was also a marked shift in the geographical distribution of exports. Turkey has overcome the problem of slow growth of OECD markets, accompanied at times by barriers against Turkish exports, by a rapid expansion of sales to countries in the Middle East and North Africa. Exports to these countries accounted for 72 percent of the increase of total exports in 1981 and 63 percent in 1982. In consequence, the share of these countries rose from 22 percent in 1980 to 45 percent during 1982, while that of the OECD fell from 58 to 45 percent. Turkish exports to Iran and Iraq rose particularly fast. Their combined share increased from 7.5 percent in 1980 to 24 percent in 1982. Turkey has stepped up exports to other countries in this area, partly in response to efforts to create better conditions for trade through bilateral cooperation agreements. This has lessened the risk of reliance on only a small number of markets. Thus, the decline of exports to Libya in 1982, owing to her payment difficulties, was compensated by increased sales to Algeria and Egypt.

The figures for 1983 indicate that Iran continues to be Turkey's largest export market, while West Germany continues second largest. Italy, Saudi Arabia and Iraq follow in terms of magnitude. The volume of exports to Iraq has fallen, a reflection of Iraq's financial difficulties.

Major Export Markets
1982-83
($ million)

	1983	1982	Percentage Change
Iran	1,087	791	+37.5
W. Germany	837	707	+18.4
Italy	422	327	+29.1
Saudi Arabia	364	357	+2.0
Iraq	319	610	-47.7

Export figures for the first quarter of 1984 have been encouraging. They indicate increases of 13.2, 48.9 and 49.5 percent for January, February and March over the corresponding months of 1983 in dollar terms. This suggests that the exchange rate liberalization policy, which resulted in a cheaper lira and therefore cheaper Turkish exports, may have borne fruit. Indeed, if the first quarter 1984 total of $1.854 billion is repeated in subsequent quarters, the government will not be far from its avowed goal of raising Turkish exports to $8 billion annually.

10.4 IMPORTS. While exports rose substantially, imports expanded only moderately in 1981 and 1982. Following a 56 percent increase in dollar terms in 1980, the increase in the total value of imports was contained at 23 percent in 1981 and less than 1 percent in 1982. The fall in dollar prices of industrial imports can be explained by the fact that most industrial imports originate from countries whose currencies depreciated against the U.S. dollar during this period, and by the reduction of the risk premium built into prices as the Turkish foreign payments situation normalized.

The figures for 1983 indicate that Iran rose to be Turkey's largest supplier (from being the fifth in the previous year). West Germany followed, then Iraq (the largest supplier in 1982), then Libya, then the United States.

Major Suppliers
1982-83
($ million)

	1983	1982	Percentage Change
Iran	1,222	747	+63.4
W. Germany	1,052	1,009	+4.9
Iraq	946	1,417	-33.2
Libya	793	823	-3.6
United States	695	813	-14.4

The figures for the first quarter of 1984 indicate declining imports. The figures for January, February and March were 9.4, 7.3 and 4.5 percent lower respectively than the corresponding months in 1983. This trend indicates that despite higher inflation, the declining Turkish lira is stemming the demand for imports. It also implies that the recent expansion in the range of goods Turkey imports may not, after all, result in dramatic shifts against domestically produced alternatives.

10.5 INVISIBLES. Net invisible earnings attained $2.1 billion in 1981, but fell to $1.9 billion in 1982. Interest payments have picked up sharply in 1981 and 1982 because of increasing external debt and rising interest rates, attaining $1.5 billion in 1982. After a sharp rise in 1981, worker remittances fell by 13 percent in dollar terms in 1982. This reflects not only a rise in the exchange rate of the dollar against the currencies of host countries, particularly the Deutschmark, but also slower wage increases and rising unemployment.

Net tourism receipts continue to be negatively affected by the lack of infrastructure, but it is also likely that some tourism earnings are recorded as worker remittances because of attractive conditions of remuneration offered by the banking system. In contrast, receipts of "other" net invisibles increased from less than $200 million in 1980 to $560 million in 1981 and $941 million in 1982, owing to the rapid growth of transit trade and rising remittances of profits from Turkish contracting firms working abroad. The latter have become very active in construction in the Middle East and North Africa, with an estimated $17 billion on their order books at present.

The figures for 1983 indicate a definite drop in workers' remittances from abroad. The cumulative total for the first ten months of 1983 was $1.326 billion, a 28 percent decline from the corresponding period of 1982. That this occurred despite the fall in the value of the lira (which should have made transfers more attractive) suggests that economic pressures abroad are putting a limit on the volume of remittances to be expected from workers abroad.

10.6 TOURISM. The tourist potential of Turkey, despite policy declarations in its favor, remains largely unexploited. Turkey has much to offer both for package tourism and the more sophisticated traveler. Turkey should be able to earn as much foreign exchange from tourism as Greece or Yugoslavia, which earned $1.9 and $1.3 million, respectively, in 1981. This would go a long way toward correcting the country's still vulnerable balance of payments position; it could also help significantly to reduce the number of unemployed.

In 1981 Turkey earned only $381 million, yet this was the highest figure ever achieved until that point. In 1982 it fell to $370 million. The number of foreign tourists is estimated to have risen to 1.6 million in 1983 (from 1.3 million in 1982), and revenue from tourism is estimated at a record $450 million for 1983.

There are various reasons for the low earnings in this sector. Apart from inadequate bed-capacity (only 10 percent of Turkey's 300,000 hotel beds are considered suitable by European standards), it seems that the approach to developing foreign tourism has been handicapped by local attitudes and the inflexibility of institutions (both private and public). Tourism should be seen as a high-potential service industry, and should be given the administrative and physical facilities to develop.

The state-owned Tourism Bank is the biggest hotel group operator, with thirteen hotels and a travel agency. It also provides credit for private sector tourist schemes on generous terms, but demand seems limited. In 1983, only $20.1 million was disbursed out of the Tourism Bank's budget of $32.2 million. For 1984, the Tourism Bank expects to lend only $28.1 million out of its projected $50.2 million budget.

10.7 CAPITAL FLOWS. The financing of the current account in 1981 and 1982 has continued to be dominated by official capital inflows, organized following Turkey's payment crisis of 1977. With the narrowing of the current account deficit, official inflows, which had been as high as $2.1 billion in 1980, were reduced to $1.5 billion in 1981 and $1.8 billion in 1982. Prominent among these were the OECD Special Assistance Program and World Bank loans.

Private capital inflows (net) resulting from foreign direct investment have been relatively small, averaging some $50 million in the last three years. However, the interest of foreign firms in investing in Turkey has been rising as a result of the more liberal attitude toward foreign investors since 1980. This has been helped by using Turkish lira counterparts of the rescheduled non-guaranteed foreign trade debt for capital increases and fixed investment.

After the rescheduling of Turkey's foreign debt in 1979 and 1980, debt repayments amounted to $585 million in 1981 and $700 million in 1982. The errors and ommissions item has been positive and usually large in 1980 and 1981, possibly indicating the inflow of substantial amounts of short-term commercial credits. Since 1978, the Turkish authorities have drawn on IMF credit under successive stand-by arrangements.

Turkey is a major recipient of aid from the United States, a reflection of the strategic value of Turkey as an American ally. The proposed allocation for 1985 is a total of $934 million: $275 million in grants for military purchases, $250 million in general grants, $230 million in military grants, and $179 million in other grants and loans (mostly through the Economic Support Fund). Turkey is reported to have requested aid from Saudi Arabia, capitalizing on the latter's preference for Muslim aid recipients. The total amount Evren is said to have requested on a recent trip to Saudi Arabia is $6 billion. Turkey has raised a total of $125.5 million in syndicated loans supplied by Islamic governments and quasi-governmental institutions in the first quarter of 1984, including a $35 million Islamic Development Bank loan.

11.
POLITICAL FACTORS AND FOREIGN BUSINESS

11.1 OUTLOOK. Progress in the Turkish economy is obvious, and is likely to continue. Foreign investors are welcomed both by the government and the country's major industrial groups. Turkey is now the most stable country in the eastern Mediterranean. With its 46 million people (estimated population in the year 2000 is 70 million), Turkey has a large domestic market. Moreover, for foreign business, the country can easily be used as a springboard for the Middle East and North African markets.

11.2 FOREIGN INVESTMENT. A recent OECD survey of nearly 100 foreign and Turkish firms, banks and organizations dealing with foreign investment showed nearly unanimous consensus that the climate for investment in Turkey has improved considerably since 1980.

Of the foreign firms operating in Turkey, 90 percent said they plan new investments for extension or modernization. Most of those surveyed were convinced that a profound change of direction is taking place in the Turkish economy: from protectionism, with emphasis on state control and import substitution, to market orientation with emphasis on private enterprise and export stimulation.

Non-petroleum foreign investment in the Turkish Republic from 1958, when a law was passed to encourage foreign investment, totaled only $314 million through 1980. This total figure was surpassed in 1981 alone, when $337 million was invested. In 1982, the figure was $167 million.

The major countries investing in Turkey are the Federal Republic of Germany (38 firms), Switzerland (37 firms), and the United States (25 firms). The number of foreign enterprises and jointly-owned ventures in Turkey was 170 at the end of 1982, with a total nominal capital of $500 million. A recent trend has been the growing number of Arab-Turkish joint ventures, and increased financing of industrial investment by the Islamic Development Bank (of which Turkey is a member) through direct participation.

The burst of investment activity during the last three years was due largely to the opportunity to buy unguaranteed trade arrears in Turkish currency and use them for capital investment. However, the period for the use of such funds has ended.

The Ozal government has taken effective measures to encourage foreign investment. Foreign companies bringing in a minimum $50,000 are now permitted to invest in any sector of their choice, and to repatriate profits (including profits from local shareholding or capital liquidation) at the going exchange rate.

11.3 STABILITY. Chances for reasonable political stability look good. The new constitution and the law governing elections and political activity are designed to bring order to Turkey's previously fractious democracy. The constitution is conservative in restricting union activities and allowing for compulsory arbitration of labor disputes.

For the foreign business community, the outlook for the forseeable future is good. The elections resulted in a conservative government determined to maintain good relations with President Evren and the business world. The government sees foreign investment as an aid in dealing with Turkey's economic problems. It will continue to strengthen the Foreign Investment Department, which was set up in the State Planning Organization, and is expected to introduce new legislation to cut red tape, particularly in customs and currency regulations.

IV. TURKEY: STATISTICAL APPENDIX

Table 1.

BASIC INFORMATION

Official name: Republic of Turkey

Country Abbreviation: TU

Date of Independence: A republic was declared Oct. 29, 1923

National Flag: A white crescent and star on red field.

National Emblem: An elliptical red shield bearing the republic's name in gold at the top with a white crescent beneath it and a white star in the center. The Turkish national colors are red and white.

National Anthem Title: Istiklal Marsi ("The March of Independence")

National Holidays: January 1, April 23, May 1, 19, 27, August 30, October 29
Muslim holidays depend on the sightings of the moon.

Weights and Measures: The Metric System prevails.

Time: GMT +3

Currency units: The Turkish Lira is divided into 100 kurus (piastres). Coins in general circulation: 25 and 50 kurus; 1, 2 1/2, and 5 Lira.

Languages: Turkish, Kurdish, Armenian, Greek

N.B. The Turkish letter **C** is pronounced like the English J in jam. In the interest of textual clarity, Turkish words and names are presented without diacritical marks.

Geographic Facts:

Area: 779,452 sq. km.
Capital City: Ankara
Total population (1982): 46,312,000
Population (1980 census): 1,877,755

Nature of Government: Restricted Democracy

Date of Constitution: July 9, 1961 Constitution was abolished by the National Security Council, and revised and ratified November 1982.

Foreign Policy Position: Pro-Western

Table 2.

CABINET LIST
(December 13, 1983)

President and Chief of the General Staff	General Kenan Evren
Prime Minister	Turgut Ozal
Deputy Prime Minister	Kaya Erdem
Deputy Prime Minister for Economic Affairs	Turgut Ozal
Minister of Justice	Necat Eldem
Minister of Defence	Zeki Yavuzturk
Minister of Foreign Affairs	Vahit Halefoglu
Minister of Finance	Vural Arikan
Minister of Education	Vehbi Dincerler
Minister of the Interior	Ali Tanriyar
Minister of Trade	Cahit Aral
Minister of Health and Social Welfare	Mehmet Aydin
Minister of Customs and Monopolies	Vural Arikan
Minister of Agriculture and Forestry	Husnu Dogan
Minister of Labor	Mustafa Kalemli
Minister of Industry and Technology	Cahit Aral
Minister of Energy and Natural Resources	Cemal Buyukbas
Minister of Culture and Tourism	Mukerrem Tascioglu
Minister of Housing and Reconstruction	Safa Giray
Minister of Rural Affairs	Husnu Dogan
Minister of Youth and Sports	Vehbi Dincerler
Minister of Social Security	Mehmet Aydin

Ministers of State: Kazim Oksay, Mesut Yilmaz, Sudi N. Turel, Abdullah Tenekeci, Ismail Ozdaglar, Ahmet K. Alptemocin.

Past Presidents:

Mustafa Kemal Ataturk	Oct 29, 1923-Nov 10, 1938
Ismet Inonu	Nov 11, 1938-May 21, 1950
Celal Bayar	May 22, 1950-May 27, 1960
Cemal Gursel	Oct 26, 1961-Mar 27, 1966
Cevdet Sunay	Mar 29, 1966-Mar 28, 1973
Fahri S. Koruturk	Apr 6, 1973-Apr 6, 1980
Kenan Evran	Sept 1980- present

Table 3.

POLITICAL PARTIES [1]

Party	Current Leader	Description
Great Turkey Party	Husmamettin Cindoruk	Reconstituted Justice Party; banned 31 May 1983.
National Democratic Party*	Gen. Turgut Sunalp	Had backing of military government.
Motherland Party*!	Turgut Ozal	Traditional nationalist.
New Order Party	Vahap Esendag	
Noble Duty Party	Aha Vefa Karatay	
Our Party	Mithat Ceylan	
Populist Party*	Necdet Calp	Had backing of military government.
Renaissance Party	Sezai Adkag	
Republican Conservative Party	Mehmet Hamak	
True Path Party	Ahmet Nusret Tuna	
Social Democratic Party	Prof. Erdal Inonu	Aimed to draw support from former Republican People's Party; banned 24 June 1983.
Virtue Party	Alparslan Demirel	

! Won the National elections
* One of the three government-approved parties

---

[1] In May 1983 new political parties were permitted under strict rules. The former political parties regrouped under new names and with new leaders. Within a month, two major new parties, the Great Turkey Party and the Social Democratic Party, had been banned.

At the time of the general election (6 November 1983) only three of the newly organized parties had gained government approval. All other parties were disqualified.

Table 4.

MEMBERSHIP IN INTERNATIONAL ORGANIZATIONS

United Nations (Turkey is a founding member)
 Share of UN budget: 0.3%.
 Permanent Representative of Turkey to the UN: A. Coskun Kirca

United Nations Development Programme – UNDP
 UNDP Representative: Sarfraz Khan Malik
 UNDP Indicative Planning Figures for Projects in Turkey:
  1977-81: $20,000,000
  1982-86: $20,000,000

United Nations Relief and Works Agency for Palestine Refugees in the Near East – UNRWA

North Atlantic Treaty Organization – NATO

International Bank for Reconstruction and Development – IBRD
 Total loans, 1947-June 1982: 51. Value: $3,777.2 million
 Approved Bank Loans, July 1981-June 1982:
  $100.0 million for development finance companies
  $88.1 million for water supply and sewerage

International Development Association – IDA
 Development Credits as of June 1982: 10; Value: $178.5 million

International Finance Corporation – IFC
 Total Cumulative IFC Investment in Turkey to 30 June 1981:
  18 enterprises; $225,584,000

Islamic Development Bank – IDB
 Turkish Subscription (August 1982): 63.1 million Islamic Dinars

Organization of the Islamic Conference – OIC
 Subsidiary Organs based in Turkey:
  Research Centre for Islamic History, Art and Culture: Istanbul f. 1976
  Statistical, Economic and Social Research and Training for the Islamic Countries: Ankara, f. 1977

Regional Cooperation for Development (Iran, Pakistan, Turkey)

International Union for Oriental and Asian Studies

U.S. ambassador to Turkey: Robert Strauz-Hupe
Turkish ambassador to U.S.: Dr. Sukru Elekdag

DEFENSE

Table 5.

TURKISH MILITARY PERSONNEL AND EQUIPMENT

Chief of General Staff: General Nurettin Ersin
Army Commander: General Necdet Urug
Navy Commander: Admiral Nejat Tumer
Air Force Commander: General Tahsin Sahinkaya

Type of Military Service: 20 months compulsory service for males.

Defense expenditure 1982: $3,375,000,000

Armed Forces

Army: 470,000 (420,000 conscripts)

4 army HQ: 10 corps HQ.
2 mechanized infantry divisions
14 infantry divisions
6 armed brigades
4 mechanized brigades
11 infantry brigades
1 parachute brigade, 1 commando brigade
4 surface-to-surface battalions with Honest John
Independent units: 8 armed reconnaissance, 32 artillery, 8 anti-aircrart artillery battalions, fortress defense regiments
Armored fighting vehicles: 77 Leopard 1A3, 500 M-47, 3,000 M-48 main battle tanks; 2,000 M-113 armored personnel carriers
Artillery: 150 M-59 155 mm towed, 36 M-107 175mm self-propelled guns; 95 M-116A1 75mm pack, some 140 M-101A1 105mm, 400 M-114A1 155mm, 116 M-115 203mm towed, 400 M-7/M-108 105mm, M-44 155mm, 48 M-110 203mm self-propelled how; 1,750 60mm, 81mm, 4.2-in (107mm) and 120mm mortars; 18 Honest John surface-to-surface missiles
Anti-tank: 1,200 57mm, 390 75mm, 800 106mm RCL; 85 Cobra, SS-11, TOW anti-tank guided weapons
Anti-aircraft: 300 twin 20mm, 900 40mm, M-51 75mm, M-117/M-118 90 mm guns.
Air: 2 DHC-2, 18 U-17, 6 Cessna 206, 3 Cessna 421, 15 Do-27, 9 Do-28, 20 Baron, 5 T-42, 40 Citabria 150S training aircraft; 156 AB-204/-205, 20 Bell 47G, 48 UH-1D, 30 TH-300C helicopters
(On order: TOW, 2,500 Milan anti-tank guided weapons, 27 UH-1H helicopter)

Reserves: 700,000

Navy: 46,000 including marines (36,000 conscripts)

18 combat aircraft
7 combat helicopters
16 submarines (2 reserve): 5 Type 209, 10 U.S. Guppy, 1 Tang (on loan)
15 U.S. destroyers: 9 Gearing (3 leased, 5 with 1 X 8 ASROC),
2 Fletcher, 2 Sumner, 2 Carpenter 2 Berk frigates, each with helicopter
13 fast attack craft (missile): 4 Dogan (Lurssen FPB-57) with 2 X 4 Harpoon surface-to-surface missile; 9 Kartal (Type 141 Jaguar) with 4 Penguin II SSM
8 fast attack craft (torpedo): 7 frigates Jaguar, 1 Girne.
21 large patrol craft: (including 2 U.S. Asheville, 6 PC-1638, 4 PGM-71)
4 83-ft coastal patrol craft, 1 Nusret, 6 coastal minelayers
26 minesweepers: 12 U.S. Adjutant, 4 Canadian MCB,
6 FGR Vegesack coastal, 4 U.S. Cape inshore
5 landing ships, tank (3 dual-purpose minelayers), 31 landing crafts, tank, 16 landing crafts, utility, 20 landing crafts, mechanized
56 auxiliary ships including 1 U.S. destroyer tender, 1 frigate depot ship (training) 9 tankers (5 fleet)
1 anti-submarine warfare squadron: 18 S-2E aircraft; 3 AB-204B, 4 AB-212 anti-submarine warfare helicopter (2 S-2A in reserve)
1 marine brigade (5,000): HQ, 3 battalions, 1 artillery battalion (with 18 guns), support units

(On order: 1 Type 209 submarine, 4 Meko-200 frigates, 2 Lurssen fast attack craft [missile], 13 landing craft [tank], Harpoon surface-to-surface missile)

Bases: Golcuk, Istanbul, Izmir, Eregli, Iskenderun.

Reserves: 70,000

Air Force: 53,000 (33,000 conscripts); 340 combat aircraft

2 tactical, 1 administrative, and 1 air training commands
13 fighter, ground attack squadrons: 2 with 42 F-5A, 12 F-5B; 2 with 40 F-100C/D/F; 6 with 82 F- 4E, 8 RF-4E; 3 with 50 F/TF-104G.
2 interceptor squadrons with 30 F-104S.
1 reconnaissance squadron with 17 RF-5A/F-5B.
6 transport squadrons: 2 with 7 C-130E, 20 C-160D; 3 with 30 C-47A; 1 (vip) with 3 Viscount 794, 2 Islander aircraft, 12 UH-1D/H, 5 UH-19D helicopter
1 VIP flight with 2 C-47A.
9 base flights with 40 T-33A, 2 C-47A aircraft, 2 UH-1H helicopters operational conversion units with 36 F-100C/F, 20 F/TF-104.
3 training squadrons with 24 T-34A, 25 T-37B/C, 60 T-38A, 20 T-41D.

Air Force (cont.)

Air-to-air missiles: Sidewinder, 750 AIM-9P3 Super Sidewinder, Sparrow, Falcon, Shafrir
Air-to surface missiles: AS-12, Bullpup, Maverick
8 surface-to-air missiles squadrons with 72 Nike Hercules

(On order: 33 F-104G aircraft; UH-1H helicopter (10 search and rescue, 4 electronic counter measures); Super Sidewinder, Sparrow air-to-air missile)

Reserves: 66,000

Forces Abroad: Cyprus: 1 corps of 2 infantry divisions (17,000); 150 M-47/-48 MBT; M-113 armored personnel carrier; 212 105mm, 155mm, 203mm guns/howitzers; 40mm anti-aircraft guns

Para-Military Forces: Gendarmerie 125,000 (including 3 mobile brigades with Commando armored personnel carriers), 30+ large patrol craft
(On order: 5 SAR-33 fast attack craft)

Source: The Military Balance 1983-84

Table 6.

UNITED STATES MILITARY ASSISTANCE TO TURKEY, 1946-1980
(million US $)

1979	180.3
Credit Sales	175.0
Grants	5.3
1980	208.3
Credit Sales	202.9
Grants	5.4
Total Loans & Grants 1946-1980	5,377.4
Credit Sales	987.9
Grants	4,389.5

Source: Agency for International Development

Table 7.

TURKISH MILITARY EXPENDITURES

Year	Military Expenditure (billion US $)	% of GNP	% of Central Govt. Expend.
1978	2.281	5.1	19.1
1979	2.035	4.2	14.7
1980	2.166	4.2	16.6
1981	2.814	4.6	20.0
1982	3.375	5.2	NA

Source: World Military Expenditures and Arms Transfers 1972-1982
U.S. Arms Control and Disarmament Agency

Table 8.

ARMS IMPORTS AND EXPORTS
(current million US $)

	Imports	Exports
1978	220	10
1979	170	10
1980	290	150
1981	340	150
1982	420	160

Source: World Military Expenditures and Arms Transfers 1972-1982
U.S. Arms Control and Disarmament Agency

Table 9.

VALUE OF ARMS TRANSFERS BY MAJOR SUPPLIER
(Cumulative 1978-82 current $mn)

Total	**1,400**
United States	750
France	10
West Germany	500
Italy	110
Others	80

Source: World Military Expenditures and Arms Transfers 1972-1982
U.S. Arms Control and Disarmament Agency.

Table 10.

REGISTER OF WARSHIPS ON ORDER FROM WEST GERMANY
(as of March 1, 1983)

Year	Number ordered	Designation	Comments
1974	(8)	Type 209 Submarines	Licence-produced in Turkey; in addition to 4 delivered directly from FRG
1976	13	SAR-33 Type Fast attack craft	Prototype delivered from FRG for trials in 1977; rest being built in Turkey
1979	1	Type 57 Fast attack craft	In addition to 4 in service also designated Dogan-class
1982	4	Meko-200 Destroyers, Frigates, Corvettes	Two licence-produced in Golcuk, Turkey

Source: SIPRI 1983

Table 11.

TURKISH ARMS SALES TO THE MIDDLE EAST

1 tank landing ship ordered by Libya
1 SAR-33 patrol craft ordered by Libya in 1980

Source: SIPRI Yearbook 1982

Table 12.

TRADE IN MAJOR CONVENTIONAL WEAPONS

Supplier	No. ordered	Weapon designation	Weapon description	Year of order	Year of delivery	No. delivered
Belgium						
	18	F-104G	Fighter	1981	1981	3
					1982	15
Egypt						
	35	F-4E Phantom	Fighter	(1982)		
West Germany						
	1	Dogan Class	FAC	1979		
	(4)	Leopard ARV	ARV	1980	1981	(2)
	77	Leopard-1-A3	MBT	1980	1982	(20)
	4	Meko-200	Frigate	1982		
	(2,500)	Milan	ATM	1981	1981	480
Netherlands						
	25	F-104G	Fighter	1980	1981	(10)
USA						
	750	AIM-9P	AAM	1982		
		BGM-71A TOW	ATM	(1979)		
	15	F-4E Phantom	Fighter	1981		
	1	Gearing Class	Destroyer	(1980)		
	25	Model 205 UH-1H	Helicopter	1981		
	12	RGM-84A Harpoon	ShShM	1980		

Source: SIPRI Yearbook 1983

DEMOGRAPHY

Table 13.

CHIEF DEMOGRAPHIC INDICATORS
(1982)

Population, total (in thousands) (1981):	45,529.0
(1982 mid-year estimate):	46,312.0
Population, males (in 1,000):	23,050.5
Population, females (in 1,000):	22,295.3
Population ages (% of total)	
0-4:	14.72
5-14:	23.90
15-64:	57.0
65+:	4.4
Population under 20 as % of total:	49.62
Women ages 15-49 as % of total:	47.95
Dependency ratios (per 1,000):	760.6
Child-woman ratios (per 1):	0.624
Median age (years):	20.19
Divorce rate (per 1,000):	0.3
Urban population as % of total (1982 estimate):	44.7%
Population density (per sq km):	56.9
Crude birth rates (per 1000 pop.):	33.2
Crude death rates (per 1000 pop.):	9.2
Rates of growth (%):	2.477
Gross reproduction rates:	2.420
Net reproduction rates:	2.014
Total fertility rates (per 1000):	4,961.0
Life expectancy, total: (years)	62.4
Life expectancy, male:	60.4
Life expectancy, female:	64.4
Total fertility rate:	4.6

Source: World Tables: World Bank, Social Data 1983; UN Demographic Yearbook 1982.

Table 14.

POPULATION OF PRINCIPAL TOWNS

Principal towns	**Population**
Ankara (capital) *	1,877,755
Istanbul	2,772,708
Izmir (Smyrna) *	757,854
Adana	574,515
Bursa	445,113
Gaziantep	374,290
Konya	329,139
Eskisehir	309,431
Kayseri	281,320
Diyarbakir	235,617
Mersin (Icel)	216,308
Samsun	198,749
Izmit (Kocaeli)	190,423
Erzurum	190,241
Malatya	179,074
Kahramanmaras	178,557
Kirikkale	178,401
Kagrthane	175,540
Antalya	173,501
Sivas	172,864

* Within municipal boundaries

Source: 1980 National Census

ECONOMY

Table 15.

FINANCIAL SURVEY

International Liquidity
(million US $)

	1979	1980	1981	1982	1983	1984+
Total Reserves minus Gold	767	1,274	1,285	923	1,270	1,164
Foreign Exchange	767	1,274	1,285	923	1,235	1,125
Gold (million fine troy ounces)	3.765	3.768	3.768	3.769	3.775	3.776
Gold (national valuation)	159	159	159	159	159	159
Central Bank: Other Liabilities	5,544	7,086	6,160	6,047	6,228*	NA
US Liabilities to Turkey	225	242	526	296	471	321
US Claims on Turkey	189	187	477	696	846	992

Commercial Banks
(billion TL)

	1979	1980	1981	1982	1983
Claims on Government	41.6	68.3	158.6	384.1	367.3*
Claims on Private Sector	380.8	660.3	1,231.3	1,813.5	2,230.0*
Claims on Govt Enterprises	78.0	159.0	160.8	156.2	202.7*
Claims on Other Financial Institutions	2.3	2.3	2.7	12.0	12.5*
Foreign Assets	9.1	49.3	106.1	177.4	224.6*
Reserves	150.5	219.5	429.2	592.2	659.8*
Foreign Liabilities	2.8	7.4	6.2	64.1	103.7*
Demand Deposits	297.6	481.5	681.2	923.8	934.5*
Time and Saving Deposits	84.3	181.9	672.7	1,217.4	1,311.9*
Government Deposits	50.9	84.1	157.4	218.5	264.2*
Capital Accounts	51.9	81.2	80.1	173.5	231.5*
Other Items (Net)	72.3	93.3	-5.4	-174.7	-73.8*

+ 1984 2nd quarter figures
* 1983 3rd quarter figures

Source: International Financial Statistics July, 1984

FINANCIAL SURVEY

Central Bank
(billion TL)

	1979	1980	1981	1982	1983
Foreign Assets	59.1	270.3	495.8	807.7	1,126.2*
Claims on Government	262.4	630.9	993.1	1,349.2	1,575.3*
Claims on Govt Enterprises	123.7	180.2	236.0	260.8	254.8*
Claims on Deposit Money Banks	213.7	316.8	420.1	377.0	413.5*
Claims on Other Fin Inst.	47.2	48.7	53.7	66.9	73.9*
Reserve Money	309.4	457.7	717.2	1,011.2	1,104.3*
Foreign Liabilities	218.3	733.8	999.7	1,401.1	1,931.2*
Government Deposits	5.3	49.0	269.1	301.1	267.1*
Capital Accounts	9.2	17.4	25.9	38.7	40.3*
Other Items (Net)	3.4	19.8	-9.6	22.8	2.5*

Monetary Survey
(billion TL)

	1979	1980	1981	1982	1983
Foreign Assets (Net)	-153.0	-421.6	-404.0	-480.2	-684.0*
Domestic Credit	879.9	1,616.6	2,409.9	3,523.1	4,185.2*
Claims on Government (Net)	247.8	566.1	725.3	1,213.8	1,411.3*
Claims on Govt Enterprises	201.7	339.2	396.8	416.9	457.5*
Claims on Private Sector	380.8	660.3	1,231.3	1,813.5	2,230.0*
Claims on Other Fin Inst.	49.6	51.0	56.5	78.9	86.4*
Money	465.5	719.8	969.3	1,342.7	1,378.9*
Quasi-Money	85.5	183.1	736.9	1,220.3	1,313.3*
Government Lending Funds	11.5	33.3	104.9	228.7	246.2*
Other Items (Net)	173.5	258.8	194.8	250.3	562.7*

Table 16.

GROSS DOMESTIC PRODUCT BY SECTORAL ORIGIN
(1968 Prices)

	1977	1978	1979	1980	1981	1982
Agriculture	42,180	43,302	44,518	45,268	45,423	48,470
Crops & livestock	41,000	41,874	42,985	43,622	43,681	46,796
Forestry	805	988	994	1,015	1,058	941
Fishing	375	440	539	631	684	733
Industry	43,145	45,991	43,429	40,887	43,834	45,223
Mining & quarrying	4,411	5,590	4,678	4,163	4,264	3,526
Manufacturing	35,547	36,818	34,881	32,991	35,662	37,386
Electricity, gas & water	3,187	3,583	3,869	3,733	3,908	4,311
Construction	11,783	12,271	12,786	12,885	12,939	13,002
Wholesale & retail trade	26,413	27,448	26,813	25,701	28,211	29,854
Transport, storage & communications	19,023	19,502	18,642	17,971	18,668	18,916
Banking, insurance & other financial institutions	4,566	4,785	4,929	5,018	5,113	5,261
Ownership of dwellings	8,818	9,174	9,528	9,921	10,185	10,453
Private services	9,241	9,536	9,449	9,353	9,775	10,224
Government services	17,546	18,629	19,416	20,546	21,367	22,521
Gross domestic product at factor cost	182,716	190,639	189,509	187,550	195,514	203,925
Indirect taxes less subsidies	18,861	16,675	15,977	16,406	17,395	19,066
Gross domestic product at 1968 market prices	201,577	207,314	205,486	203,956	212,909	222,991
Net factor income from abroad	1,781	1,869	2,857	2,165	1,831	1,252
GROSS NATIONAL PRODUCT AT 1968 MARKET PRICES	**203,358**	**209,183**	**208,343**	**206,121**	**214,740**	**224,243**

Source: State Institute of Statistics; State Planning Organization

Table 17.

CONSOLIDATED COMMERCIAL BANK CREDITS
(million TL)

	1977	1978	1979	1980	1981	1982*
By economic sectors:						
Industry	99,155	119,158	156,360	283,108	459,295	504,816
Agriculture	49,135	52,854	82,599	145,780	265,957	267,624
Foreign trade and tourism	16,309	21,107	28,108	60,724	127,092	400,465
Housing and other construction	11,201	14,321	16,869	18,450	32,404	45,686
Artisans and small traders	9,516	13,707	23,088	37,239	62,926	87,246
Distribution and services	52,972	75,193	139,164	244,214	370,393	264,482
Investment and development banks	0	0	0	0	0	2,393
Insurance Companies	0	0	0	0	621	372
Total	**238,288**	**296,340**	**446,188**	**789,515**	**1,318,688**	**4,573,084**
By public and private sectors:						
Public enterprises	30,124	33,737	65,119	138,013	142,707	118,902
Public administrations	7,460	9,657	10,935	10,691	17,463	14,856
Private enterprises and households	200,704	252,946	370,134	640,811	1,157,897	1,436,561
Other financial institutions	0	0	0	0	621	2.765
Total	**238,288**	**296,340**	**446,188**	**789,515**	**1,318,688**	**1,573,084**

* Estimate

Source: Central Bank

Table 18.

EXCHANGE RATES: LIRAS PER U.S. DOLLAR
(Market Rate/Par or Central Rate, end of period)

1976	16.67
1977	19.44
1978	25.25
1979	35.35
1980	90.15
1981	133.62
1982	186.75
1983	282.80
1984	
Jan	311.47
Feb	310.29
Mar	322.69
Apr	339.64
May	357.01
June	369.94
July	382.69

Source: International Financial Statistics Sept., 1984

Table 19.

CONSUMER PRICE INDEX
Indices, 1963 = 100 (annual averages)

	1978	1979	1980	1981	1982
Wholesale prices:					
Total	751	1,231	2,551	3,488	4,369
Food and feeding stuffs:	734	1,093	2,190	3,101	3,759
Cereals	545	774	1,638	2,819	3,373
Livestock	323	1,959	3,806	4,437	5,673
Livestock products	981	1,473	2,625	3,245	4,205
Raw materials and semi-finished products:	779	1,461	3,152	4,135	5,387
Fuels	960	1,717	4,630	6,142	7,911
Minerals	645	1,353	2,735	3,302	4,585
Building materials	963	1,676	3,157	3,700	4,802
Textiles	681	1,190	2,135	2,613	3,464
Cost of living:					
Ankara, total	725	1,174	2,365	3,168	4,067
Istanbul, total	876	1,433	2,784	3,831	5,083
Food	864	1,333	2,554	3,503	4,702
Heating and lighting	096	2,122	4,404	5,302	6,454
Clothing	775	1,515	2,814	4,052	5,504
Other	958	1,616	3,386	4,802	6,113

Source: OECD Economic Surveys, Turkey 1982-1983

Table 20.

TURKISH FOREIGN DEBT
($ Million)

	1979	1980	1981	1982	1983
Medium and Long Term Debt (Disbursed)	10048	12693	13408	14092	13882
Public Sector	9689	11675	12567	13512	13274
International Organizations	1855	2213	2598	3168	3360
IBRD	890	1158	1522	1872	2249
IDA	190	184	188	174	185
IFC	100	96	73	69	54
EIB	471	447	427	420	393
ERF	148	253	287	384	399
IDB	56	60	86	190	22
OPEC Fund	-	15	15	40	40
Int'l Fund for Agr. Dev.	-	-	-	19	18
Bilateral Credits	4370	6026	6712	7115	6552
OECD countries	3976	5253	5901	6146	5613
OPEC countries	55	392	449	587	535
Other countries	339	381	362	382	404
Commercial Bank Loans	3464	3436	3257	3229	3362
Bank loans	659	763	651	720	1002
Rescheduled short term debt:					
CTID's /1	2269	2137	2077	1996	1886
Bankers credits /2	429	429	429	429	429
TPRC's /3	107	107	100	84	85
Private Sector	359	1018	841	580	601
Private Credits	359	218	241	230	258
NGTA's /4	-	800	600	350	350
Short Term Debt	3556	2480	2111	2091	2889
Public Sector	1104	1448	1154	1031	1519
Private Sector	2452	1032	957	1060	1370
Total External Debt	**13604**	**15173**	**15519**	**16183**	**16771**

/1 Reflects conversion of non-dollar denominated CTID into dollars.
/2 Bankers' credits were rescheduled in July 1979.
/3 TPRC'S have been rescheduled over three years.
/4 Amounts shown represent the dollar equivalent of obligations resheduled in 1980 as well as unfiled or unreconciled claims.

Source: Briefing Sept. 24, 1984.

Table 21.

GENERAL BUDGET ESTIMATES
Consolidated budget
(TL billion)

	1981	% Change 1981/80	1982 Budget proposal 10 months	1982 Budget proposal 12 months	1982 Outturn 10 months	1982 Outturn 12 months
Revenues	2,594		3,313	3,977	2,897	3,478
Tax revenues	1,378	60.2	1,670	2,003	1,466	1,760
Other revenues	1,189	58.7	1,449	1,739	1,303	1,564
Annex budget	27		194	235	128	154
Expenditures	1,482	39.4	1,758	2,109	1,552	1,863
Current	645	29.8	864	1,037	705	846
(Personnel)	(390)	(16.4)	(510)	(612)	(430)	(516)
Investment	290	73.6	387	464	338	406
Transfers	547	37.1	507	608	509	611
(SEEs)	(214)	(0)	(231)	(277)	(233)	(280)
Budget deficit	-104		-88	-106	-86	-103
Advance payments	-45		--		-123	
Deferred payments	111		--		93	
Cash deficit	-38		-88		-116	
Financing:						
Government bonds	23		20		54	
Treasury notes	35		45		75	
Central Bank	53		--		32	
Foreign borrowing (net)	13		23		-45	
Bank deposits	-88		--		--	
Errors and ommissions	2		--		5	

Source: OECD Economic Surveys, Turkey 1982-1983

GENERAL BUDGET ESTIMATES
Consolidated budget
(TL billion)

	% Change 1982/81	1983 Budget proposal	1983 Official forecast	% Change 1983/82*
Revenues	27.7	2,365	2,205	18.1
Tax revenues	31.5	1,980	1,980	13.9
Other revenues		344	180	
Annex budget		41	45	
Expenditures	25.6	2,505	2,265	18.8
Current	31.2	1,193	1,055	15.0
(Personnel)	(32.3)	(695)	(630)	(13.6)
Investment	40.0	555	530	19.6
Transfers	11.7	757	680	24.5
(SEEs)	(30.8)	(316)	(272)	(14.1)
Budget deficit		-140	-60	
Advance payments		--	--	
Deferred payments		--	-30	
Cash deficit		-140	-90	
Financing:				
Government bonds		135	135	
Treasury notes		-20	-30	
Central Bank		35	35	
Foreign borrowing (net)		-10	-50	
Bank deposits		--	--	
Errors and omissions		--	--	

* comparison based on proposed budget for 12 months

Table 22.

NATIONAL ACCOUNTS
(1982-provisional)
(TL million, at current prices)

Agriculture and livestock	1,672,841.1
Forestry and logging	30,129.4
Fishing	17,267.9
Mining and quarrying	169,433.1
Manufacturing	1,820,576.7
Electricity, gas and water	216,496.7
Construction	359,370.2
Wholesale and retail trade	1,356,329.4
Transport, storage and communications	798,305.2
Financial institutions	191,322.6
Ownership of dwellings	353,489.1
Other private services	445,860.8
Government services	686,597.3
Gross Domestic Product at Factor Cost	**8,118,019.5**
Indirect taxes	578,664.7
Less: Subsidies	71,248.0
GDP in Purchasers' Values	**8,625,436.2**
Net factor income from abroad	157,924.1
Gross National Product	**8,783,360.3**

Source: The Middle East and North Africa 1983-84

Table 23.

FOREIGN CAPITAL INVESTMENT BROUGHT TO TURKEY
(Million US$)

Year	**Annual Figure**	**Cumulative Figure**
1978	11.7	234.5
1979	-8.4	228.1
1980	97.0	325.1
1981	337.5	662.6
1982	167.4	830.0

Source: Turkey Economic Dialogue, special supplement, Sept 1983

Table 24.

BREAKDOWN BY COUNTRY OF FOREIGN INVESTMENT IN TURKEY
(Under Law No. 6224 as of 31st December 1982)

Country	# of firms	Total capital in TL million	Foreign capital in TL million	Foreign capital in %
FR Germany	38	16,983	8,278	49
Switzerland	37	24,763	12,372	50
USA	25	9,894	5,726	58
Netherlands	6	2,101	1,231	59
France	6	2,740	1,127	41
Italy	5	1,795	789	44
United Kingdom	5	1,689	681	40
Denmark	4	1,475	744	50
Austria	3	261	116	44
Libya	2	9,245	4,623	50
Lebanon	2	1,616	615	38
Luxembourg	2	1,471	845	57
Panama	2	420	214	51
Iran	2	290	285	98
Belgium	2	174	116	67
Japan	2	60	19	32
Sweden	2	70	6	8
Kuwait	1	590	279	47
Bahrain	1	613	490	80
Saudi Arabia	1	400	360	90
Yugoslavia	1	400	125	31
Canada	1	100	31	31
Finland	1	56	29	52
IFC	5	8,904	815	9
Islamic Development Bank	6	2,550	697	27
Mixed enterprises	8	10,761	2,237	21
Total	**170**	**99,418**	**42,848**	**43**

Source: OECD Economic Surveys, Turkey 1982-1983

Table 25.

TURKISH CONSTRUCTION ACTIVITIES IN THE MIDDLE EAST
(end 1981)

Country	Number of Firms	Value of Tenders ($ million)
Libya	88	8,000
Saudi Arabia	22	1,140
Iraq	17	772
Jordan	3	43
Abu-Dhabi	2	48
Kuwait	5	12
Egypt and Yemen	2	--
Total	**139**	**10,015**

Source: Izmir Foreign Trade Corp., "Development in Turkish Economy Performance and Prospects"; January 1982; Turkish Contractors Association; Mission Estimates

ENERGY

Table 26.

ENERGY SUPPLY AND DEMAND

	Unit	1979	1980	1981	1982	1983
Production						
crude oil	mn b	20.01	16.44	17.15	16.44	16.5*
petroleum fuels	mn t	10.0	11.2	12.0	14.8	
coal	mn t	4.1	3.6	4.0	4.0	6.8*
lignite	mn t	15.0	15.0	17.1	16.2	22.9*
other solid fuels	mn tce	7.0	7.3	6.1	6.0	6.0*
electricity	twh	22.5	23.3	24.7	26.6	27.3*
Imports						
crude oil	mn b	58.6	75.0	82.9	100.1	
petroleum fuels	mn t	4.5	3.0	2.0	1.3	
coal	mn t	0.6	0.8	0.3	1.0	
electricity	twh	1.0	1.3	1.6	1.8	
Exports						
petroleum fuels	mn t	0.04	0.1	0.3	1.2	
coal	'000 t	---	---	---	4.0	
Consumption						
petroleum fuels	mn t	14.4	13.7	13.5	14.8	
coal	mn t	4.3	4.6	4.1	5.0	5.1
lignite	mn t	14.9	15.3	16.0	16.4	
other solid fuels	mn tce	1.3	1.6	1.1	1.1	
electricity	twh	22.2	23.4	24.9	27.0	27.3

Source: United Nations * estimates

Table 27.

TURKISH CRUDE OIL IMPORTS
(figures in tons)

	1980	1981	First half 1982
Iraq	4,310,234	5,549,007	3,135,937
Iran	2,730,739	1,748,351	328,902
Saudi Arabia	304,309	1,484,187	688,067
Libya	2,580,984	2,631,858	2,227,553
Abu Dhabi	272,358	87,347	---
Algeria	---	96,993	---
Syria	69,893	---	---
Kuwait	66,115	---	---
Egypt	95,581	---	---
Total	**10,430,213**	**11,597,743**	**6,380,459**

Source: General Directorate of Petroleum Affairs

Table 28.

TURKISH OIL BALANCE

	Refinery Output	Total Product Imports	Total Product Exports	Civil Inland Consumption
1978	12,814,639	3,951,176	54,366	16,521,395
1979	10,817,516	3,513,443	53,663	14,289,639
1980	12,408,275	3,014,728	229,283	14,765,386
1981	13,107,605	2,136,108	385,277	14,665,380

Source: General Directorate of Petroleum Affairs

Table 29.

OUTPUT OF PETROLEUM, COAL, AND MAJOR MINERALS

	1978	1979	1980	1981	1982
Crude petroleum	2,759	2,831	2,330	2,363	2,333
Coal	7,741	7,200	6,599	7,388	7,161
Lignite	18,030	15,603	16,988	18,907	20,133
Chrome	669	586	551	561	607
Iron	4,198	1,955	2,523	2,954	2,596
Boron	1,320	1,172	1,334	1,000	1,381
Copper	2,092	2,204	1,589	2,516	2,648

Source: State Institute of Statistics, State Planning Organization

Table 30.

REFINED PETROLEUM PRODUCTS (1981)
('000 b/d)

	Production	Apparent Consumption	Imports
Gasoline			
Motor gasoline	49	-	0
Total gasoline (incl Aviation)	49	45	0
Kerosene and jet fuel	12	12	0
Distillate fuel oil	72	88	16
Residual fuel oil	100	116	16
Lubricants (incl greases)	3	3	1
Other	36	8	14
Refinery fuel and loss	8	8	--
Total	280	280	47

Source: International Energy Annual September 1983

Table 31.

TURKISH REFINING STATISTICS

	1980	1981	1982	1983	1984
Refining Capacity					
('000 b/d)	356	356	367	467	472
(Million t/yr)	17.7	17.7	18.2	23.1	23.5

Table 32.

PETROLEUM PRODUCT PRICES
(US dollars; TL/$=166.87)

	July 1982
(Price per gallon)	
Premium gasoline 95 RON	2.09
Regular gasoline 85 RON	1.88
Auto diesel fuel	1.27
Household kerosene	1.31
Light heating oil	1.20
LPG	.89
(Price per barrel)	
Distillate fuel oil	53.46
Marine diesel fuel	--
Medium fuel oil	39.53
Heavy fuel oil	36.57
Marine fuel oil	--

Source: International Energy Annual September 1983

Table 33.

PRODUCTION OF PETROLEUM PRODUCTS
(000 tons)

	1982	1983 (Jan-Aug.)	%Change 1983/82
Gasoline	1,948.2	1,250.9	-0.7
Kerosene	322.4	183.5	-9.5
Diesel oil	4,576.3	2,882.6	+4.1
Fuel oil	6,970.4	4,048.9	-8.2
LPG	342.0	245.7	+20.2
Others	1,925.9	1,779.3	+47.5

Source: Turkiye Is Bankasi Review of Economic Conditions 1983.

Table 34.

PRODUCTION OF ELECTRICITY (Gross)
(million kilowatt-hours)

	1977	1978	1979	1980	1981	1982
Government power plants	19,101	20,006	20,609	21,124	22,620	24,894
Thermal power	10,545	10,672	10,347	9,824	10,057	10,768
Hydro power	8,556	9,334	10,262	11,300	12,563	14,126
Industrial power plants	1,464	1,720	1,912	2,151	2,053	1,658
Thermal power	1,427	1,689	1,871	2,103	2,000	1,615
Hydro power	37	31	41	48	53	43
Total	**20,565**	**21,726**	**22,521**	**23,275**	**24,673**	**26,552**
Thermal power	11,972	12,361	12,218	11,927	12,057	12,383
Hydro power	8,593	9,365	10,303	11,348	12,616	14,169

Source: State Institute of Statistics

Table 35.

ELECTRICITY PRODUCTION AND CONSUMPTION

Year	Programmed Production	Realization	Imported (USSR & Bulgaria)
1977	20,170.0	20,564.6	492.2
1978	22,325.0	21,726.1	621.0
1979	23,320.0	22,521.9	1,044.3
1980	23,520.0	23,275.4	1,341.2
1981	25,458.0	24,673.0	1,616.0
	Available for Consumption	**Power Cutoffs**	**Demanded**
1977	21,056.8	777.0	21,833.8
1978	22,347.1	1,326.0	23,673.1
1979	23,566.2	1,625.3	25,191.5
1980	24,616.6	1,753.4	26,370.0
1981	26,289.0	1,656.0	27,945.0

Source: Turkish Electricity Authority

INDUSTRY

Table 36.

INDUSTRIAL PRODUCTION
(tons)

	1982	1983*	% Change
Public Sector			
Paper	398,102	265,994	+2.3
Cotton yarn	46,955	33,713	+9.0
Woollen yarn	4,556	3,549	+25.5
Cotton fabrics (000 meters)	234,417	158,780	+3.6
Woollen tabrics (000 meters)	6,096	4,222	+4.2
Caustic soda	42,212	25,204	+2.7
PVC (1)	39,799	31,370	+15.1
Polyethylene (1)	25,579	22,406	+28.6
Dodecyl benzene(1)	13,555	13,485	+51.4
Carbon black (1)	19,922	18,808	+43.2
Caprolactam	18,992	9,414	-32.5
Raki ('000 l)	38,866	24,788	+4.5
Beer ('000 l)	43,962	28,701	+3.2
Cigarettes	62,254	39,133	-0.7
Manufactured tobacco	1,475	788	-15.4
Sulphuric acid	18,571	11,191	+2.2
Copper	26,314	10,734	-44.0
Coke	2,101,979	1,679,023	+27.4
Public and Private Sectors			
Pig iron	2,100.3	1,776.0	+32.9
Steel ingots	1,763.4	1,171.8	+5.7
Cement	15,777.7	10,332.1	-15.2
Sugar	1,617.2	471.4	+5.8
Commercial fertilizers	5,838.0	5,296.2	+26.8
Private Sector*			
Steel mill products	240,392	202,714	+21.0
Rolling mill products	221,957	196,704	+26.2
Electrolytic copper	16,754	14,250	+22.4
Brass products	528	1,030	+229.1
Sheet aluminum	1,449	1,798	+61.0
Aluminum conductor wire	2,632	3,179	+49.5
Steel alloy conductor wire	12,118	3,491	-61.0
Sheet glass	300,228	205,950	-7.3
Bottles and glassware	195,644	158,914	+10.9

* Figures reflect production from Jan.-Aug. 1983 and % change based on comparison of 1982 and 1983 for that time period only.

Source: Turkiye Is Bankasi Review of Economic Conditions 1983

Table 37.

PRODUCTION OF SELECTED INDUSTRIAL GOODS
(Percentage change)

Sector	1979/1978	1980/1979	1981/1980	1982/1981
Mining				
Coke	16	-8	-1	11
Crude oil	4	-18	2	-1
Lignite	20	22	10	0
Coal	-6	-10	10	0
Iron ore	13	26	5	-10
Chrome	-17	5	22	7
Copper	10	-3	-5	-12
Manufacturing				
Cotton yarn	17	-7	2	11
Woollen yarn	-14	-4	15	15
Cotton fabrics	-5	-7	25	-4
Woollen fabrics	-2	-26	25	8
Sugar	3	-20	31	NA
Cigarettes	8		29	17
Paper	-4	-1	21	8
Tires	-6	9	-8	19
Fertilizer	26	32	54	-13
Synthetic rubber	53	-13	43	4
Cars	-18	-28	-20	23
Buses	34	-6	23	14
Tractors	7	16	47	40
Cement	-10	-7	17	5
Steel ingots	14	0	4	8
Steel rolled products	27	18	4	NA
Energy				
Electricity	4	4	7	7
Gasoline	-10	15	7	5
Fuel oil	-21	18	5	28

Source: OECD Economic Surveys 1982-1983 Turkey

Table 38.

TOURISTS BY COUNTRY OF ORIGIN
(thousands)

Country	1980	1981	1982
France	87	97	99
Germany, Federal Republic of	155	155	135
Greece	59	120	135
Iran	109	55	23
Italy	63	68	45
Syria	38	61	68
United Kingdom	62	60	60
USA	119	104	105
Yugoslavia	57	58	78
Total Number Foreign Arrivals	**1,288**	**1,405**	**1,391**
Receipts from foreign travel (mn US$)	326.7	381.3	370.3
Expenditures for foreign travel (mn US$)	114.8	104.2	108.9

Source: Middle East and North Africa 1983-84

Table 39.

PROGRAM OBJECTIVES AND THE REALIZED BALANCE OF TOURISM AND FOREIGN TRAVEL RECEIPTS AND EXPENDITURES 1970-1981
(million US $)

Years	Program Objectives	Realized Balance	% Rate of Change	% Rate of Realization
1970	5.0	3.9	-	78.0
1971	7.0	20.7	430.8	295.7
1972	10.0	44.4	114.5	444.0
1973	38.0	78.5	76.8	206.6
1974	94.6	41.9	-46.6	44.3
1975	124.0	46.0	9.8	37.1
1976	90.0	-27.4	-	-
1977	60.0	-63.6	-	-
1978	35.0	127.9	-	365.4
1979	200.0	185.7	45.2	92.8
1980	325.0	211.9	14.1	65.2
1981	275.0	278.0	31.2	101.1

Source: Economic Dialogue: Turkey, Special Supplement, September 1983.

Table 40.

PRODUCTION OF MAJOR METALS
('000 metric tons)

	1979	1980	1981	1982
Pig iron	1,745	2,226	1,996	2,360
Iron ore	1,956	2,260	2,100	--
Raw steel	2,396	2,536	2,425	2,800
Tinplate	72.3	74.8	63.1	101.8
Aluminum	32.1	33.6	40.4	36.3
Antimony	1.89	.969	.835	.835
Copper ore	31.4	21.3	25.4	25.0
Copper metal	23.3	15.9	26.6	25.4

Sources: Statistisches Bandesamt, W. Germany; International Tin Council World Bureau of Metal Statistics.

AGRICULTURE AND FISHING

Table 41.

PRINCIPAL LAND USE
(thousand hectares)

	1976	1977	1978	1979	1980	1981
Cultivated area	24,243	24,243	24,552	24,972	24,567	24,891
Area sown	16,321	16,531	16,352	16,605	16,379	16,687
Fallow land	7,922	7,941	8,200	8,367	8,188	8,204
Tree crops, vineyards, vegetable area	3,460	3,385	3,493	3,585	3,615	3,598
Fruit trees	1,263	1,290	1,321	1,352	1,386	1,397
Olive groves	810	816	811	812	813	833
Vineyards	768	760	790	850	820	800
Vegetable area	619	591	571	571	596	568
Forest area	20,170	20,155	20,155	20,155	20,199	20,199
Total	**47,873**	**48,012**	**48,200**	**48,712**	**48,381**	**48,688**

Source: State Institute of Statistics

Table 42.

AGRICULTURAL PRODUCTION

	1,000 tons	Percentage change over previous year				
	1982 est.	1978	1979	1980	1981	1982
Wheat	17,500	0.3	5.1	-6.0	3.0	2.9
Barley	6,300	0	10.3	1.1	11.3	6.8
Rye	420	-10.1	0	-15.3	1.0	-20.8
Maize	1,360	5.0	1.7	-2.2	-3.2	13.3
Rice	192	10.1	8.2	-29.1	38.5	-3.0
Sugar beet	11,500	-1.8	-0.9	-22.8	65.0	3.0
Soya beans	36	-40.0	0	-33.3	650.0	140.0
Figs	250	5.7	8.1	2.5	22.0	0
Grapes	3,500	9.9	0.1	2.9	2.8	-5.4
Tangerines	200	11.1	3.3	7.7	4.8	14.3
Oranges	665	0.9	3.7	2.2	-2.9	-1.5
Tea	303	13.9	23.3	-14.2	-40.3	57.8
Olives	300	172.2	-60.9	214.0	-70.3	225.0
Hazelnuts	218	6.9	-3.2	-16.7	40.0	-37.7
Tobacco	206	18.2	-25.7	7.8	-26.3	22.6
Cotton	481	-17.4	0.2	5.0	-8.4	5.0
Sunflower seeds	600	6.6	21.6	27.1	-23.3	4.3

Source: OECD Economic Surveys 1982-1983, Turkey

Table 43.

LIVESTOCK PRODUCTS
('000 metric tons)

	1979	1980	1981
Beef and veal	246*	242*	220+
Buffalo meat	24	25	25+
Mutton and lamb+	298*	295*	302+
Goats' meat+	130*	123*	125+
Pig meat+	n.a.	1	1
Horse meat+	8	7	7
Poultry meat+	228	245	256
Edible offals+	89	89	94
Tallow+	13	14	14
Cows' milk	3,386	3,421	3,600*
Buffalo milk	297	274	305*
Sheep milk	1,102	1,177	1,200*
Goats' milk	626	630	647*
Butter	119.3	117.2	122.6+
Cheese+	123.6	125.9	127.4
Hen eggs	216.1	206.7	214.4+
Honey	26.6	25.2	26.0
Wool: greasy	59.3	61.3	62.2
clean	32.6	33.0	33.6+
Cattle and buffalo hides+	45.4	47.8	47.8+
Sheep skins+	55.5	58.0	58.5+
Goat skins+	12.9	13.1	13.2+

* Unofficial figures
+ FAO estimates

Source: The Middle East and North Africa 1983-84

Table 44.

FISHING
('000 metric tons, live weight, 1980)

Inland waters	32.3
Mediterranean and Black Sea:	
Mediterranean horse mackerel	50.0
European anchovy	251.9
Other fishes	90.3
Total catch	**424.5**

Source: The Middle East and North Africa 1983-84

TRADE

Table 45.

BALANCE OF PAYMENTS (1979-1982)
(million US $)

	1979	1980	1981	1982
Current account				
Trade balance	-2,808	-4,999	-4,230	-2,988
Exports	2,261	2,910	4,703	5,746
Imports	5,069	7,909	8,933	8,734
(Oil)	(1,712)	(3,862)	(3,878)	(3,640)
(Non-oil)	(3,357)	(4,047)	(5,055)	(5,094)
Invisibles, net	1,569	1,789	2,138	1,897
Workers' remittances	1,694	2,071	2,490	2,171
Interest payments	-546	-668	-1,193	-1,471
Profit transfers	-42	-51	-56	-43
Tourism, net	179	212	277	256
Other, net	284	225	620	984
Current balance	-1,239	-3,210	-2,092	-1,091
Capital account				
Private capital	-160	313	-18	193
Imports with waiver	124	95	69	49
Direct investment	86	56	60	55
Commercial credits	-370	165	-147	89
Official capital	921	2,135	1,482	1,834
Project credits	421	547	642	754
Program credits	500	1,588	840	1,080
Debt repayments	-485	-576	-585	-787
Capital balance	276	-1,872	879	1,240
Basic balance	-963	-1,338	-1,213	149
SDR allocations	27	27	24	--
Errors and omissions	818	941	1,124	128
Overall balance	-118	-370	-65	277
Financing:				
Net use of IMF resources	8	461	335	205
Increase in liabilities	194	216	-212	70
Increase in assests (-)	-84	-307	-58	-552

Source: OECD Economic Surveys 1982-1983 Turkey

Table 46.

EXPORTS BY COMMODITIES
(million US $)

	1979	1980	1981	1982
I. **Agricultural Products**	1,344	1,672	2,219	2,141
(percent of total)	(59.4)	(57.5)	(47.2)	(37.3)
a. Cereals and pulses	164	181	326	337
b. Fruit and vegetables	648	754	795	649
Hazelnuts	353	395	302	241
Dried fruit	166	187	208	168
Citrus fruit	53	86	125	77
Other	76	86	160	163
c. Industrial crops and forestry products	448	606	813	741
Cotton	228	323	348	297
Tobacco	177	234	395	348
Other	43	49	70	96
d. Live animals and sea products	84	131	285	414
II. **Mining and Quarrying Products**	132	191	194	175
(percent of total)	(5.8)	(6.5)	(4.1)	(3.0)
a. Processed agricultural products	151	209	412	569
b. Manufactured products	634	838	1,878	2,861
Textiles and clothing	378	424	803	1,056
Hides and leather	44	50	82	111
Forestry	2	4	20	33
Chemicals	24	76	94	148
Rubber and plastics	3	16	72	60
Petroleum industry	--	39	107	343
Glass and ceramics	37	36	102	104
Cement	45	40	198	207
Iron and steel	31	34	100	362
Non-ferrous metals	14	18	30	45
Metal products and machinery	18	30	85	143
Electrical	5	11	26	75
Motor vehicles	10	50	117	110
Other	23	10	42	64
Total	**2,261**	**2,910**	**4,703**	**5,746**

Source: OECD Economic Surveys 1982-1983 Turkey

Table 47.

IMPORTS BY COMMODITIES
(million US $)

	1979	1980	1981	1982
I. Agriculture and livestock	36	50	125	176
II. Mining and quarrying	1,818	4,006	4,098	3,852
Oil	1,712	3,862	3,878	3,640
Crude oil	962	2,952	3,258	3,419
Oil products	750	910	620	221
Other	106	144	220	212
III. Industrial products	3,092	3,759	4,641	4,657
Agricultural-based processed products	115	301	229	176
Industrial products	2,977	3,458	4,412	4,657
Chemicals	524	727	919	839
Fertilizer	356	395	280	51
Rubber and plastics	145	181	240	237
Textiles	46	79	78	103
Glass and ceramics	28	35	40	34
Iron and steel	345	462	605	591
Non-ferrous metals	55	87	141	122
Metal products	14	23	23	37
Machinery	903	843	1,223	1,309
Electrical appliances	251	270	336	374
Motor vehicles	221	223	356	594
Other industrial products	89	133	171	191
IV. Imports with waiver	123	94	69	49
Total	**5,069**	**7,909**	**8,933**	**8,734**

Source: OECD Economic Surveys 1982-1983 Turkey

Table 48.

EXPORTS BY MAIN SECTORS
(thousand US $)

Year	Agriculture	%	Mining	%	Industry	%
1978	1,542,800	67.4	124,135	5.4	621,3	27.20
1979	1,343,600	59.4	132,500	5.9	785,082	34.7
1980	1,671,742	57.4	190,994	6.6	1,047,386	36.0
1981	2,219,409	47.2	193,406	4.1	2,290,119	48.7
1982	2,141,121	37.3	175,322	3.01	3,429,438	59.71

Source: Economic Dialogue Turkey Special supplement Sept. 1983

Annual growth rate, imports: 3.3% (1970-1979)
Annual growth rate, exports: 1.7% (1970-1979)

Table 49.

DIRECTION OF TRADE
(percent of total)

	1977	1978	1979	1980	1981
Exports					
Industrial Countries	69.7	64.8	63.3	56.7	46.8
Oil-Exporting Countries	8.5	8.9	9.5	13.2	32.7
Non-Oil Developing Countries	13.3	16.4	16.2	16.5	14.6
Other Countries	8.5	9.9	11.0	13.6	6.1
Imports					
Industrial Countries	68.1	60.6	59.8	45.8	47.5
Oil-Exporting Countries	20.1	22.3	21.2	37.0	38.5
Non-Oil Developing Countries	8.2	13.2	12.5	10.6	9.6
Other Countries	3.7	3.9	6.5	6.6	4.4

Source: International Financial Statistics Supplement on Trade

Table 50.

GEOGRAPHICAL DISTRIBUTION OF FOREIGN TRADE
(million US $)

	Imports				Exports			
	1980	1981	1982	1983(I)	1980	1981	1982	1983(I)
OECD Countries	3,583	4,280	4,434	--	1,680	2,264	2,556	--
EEC Countries	2,268	2,520	2,466	--	1,242	1,503	1,755	--
of which:								
France	377	400	263	61	164	216	195	41
Germany	837	940	1,009	277	604	643	707	196
Italy	300	372	415	120	218	246	327	135
United Kingdom	317	434	434	110	104	148	189	74
Other OECD Countries	1,315	1,760	1,968	--	438	761	801	--
of which:								
Japan	113	206	357	62	37	35	43	11
Switzerland	348	533	312	69	125	264	324	73
United States	442	589	814	177	127	268	252	75
Eastern Bloc	831	843	428	82	490	327	323	54
of which:								
Soviet Union	181	164	107	41	169	194	124	26
Middle East and North Africa	3,219	3,503	3,690	--	650	1,932	2,587	--
of which:								
Algeria	0	34	9	1	8	31	125	29
Egypt	24	3	1	21	20	72	145	16
Iran	802	515	748	318	85	234	791	232
Iraq	1,237	1,564	1,039	329	135	559	610	48
Jordan	20	30	10	3	48	97	105	16
Kuwait	132	107	95	29	50	71	87	15
Lebanon	16	4	6	1	73	86	112	34
Libya	778	789	919	241	60	442	235	43
Saudi Arabia	106	410	477	74	44	187	359	65
Syria	17	19	17	--	103	129	63	19
Other countries	276	307	182	--	90	180	280	--
Total:	7,909	8,933	8,734	2,349	2,910	4,703	5,746	1,358

Source: State Institute of Statistics; State Planning Organization and IFS statistics (1984)

'able 51.

TRADE WITH THE MIDDLE EAST: 1982-83
($ million)

	1982		Jan-Jun 1982		Jan-Jun 1983	
	Imports	Exports	Imports	Exports	Imports	Exports
bu Dhabi	0.4	6.6	+	4.6	0.0	1.8
lgeria	8.7	125.0	2.8	62.6	3.3	65.6
ahrain	+	1.1	+	0.8	+	0.9
ubai	+	14.6	0.0	5.6	+	7.2
gypt	0.6	145.0	0.6	71.3	21.2	41.1
ran	747.7	791.0	219.6	238.4	572.9	520.8
raq	1,309.4	610.4	809.3	403.2	483.1	98.3
ordan	7.5	104.7	4.2	31.1	8.5	38.4
uwait	92.4	87.0	31.4	35.8	40.9	34.3
ebanon	2.9	111.6	2.1	48.9	1.1	61.1
ibya	919.4	234.6	453.1	140.7	408.2	111.0
man	0.0	2.7	0.0	0.5	+	+
atar	0.0	4.0	0.0	1.2	5.7	2.8
audi Arabia	477.2	358.0	175.7	119.1	129.9	134.5
udan	+	5.8	0.0	1.9	0.0	2.3
yria	14.2	63.1	12.9	33.2	1.0	34.9
unisia	17.7	24.4	8.1	12.1	21.3	27.5
thers	274.2	166.2	43.7	46.2	64.2	40.8
otal	3,872.3	2,855.8	1,763.5	1,257.162	1,759.289	1,223.350

Less than $100,000
'otals may be inexact because of rounding

ource: MEED Nov. 1983 p.10

'able 52.

FOREIGN TRADE INDICATORS

	1976	1977	1978	1979	1980	1981
atio of exports to GDP	4.7	3.6	4.3	3.5	5.1	8.3
atio of imports to GDP	12.6	12.2	8.9	8.2	13.7	15.8
atio of exports to imports	0.38	0.30	0.50	0.45	0.38	0.52
'erms of trade (1975=100)	102.7	102.2	95.0	94.8	75.3	-

ource: International Financial Statistics Trade Supplement

LABOR

Table 53.

LABOR FORCE, EMPLOYMENT AND UNEMPLOYMENT
(In thousands)

	1978	1979	1980	1981	1982
Total civilian labor force	17,525	17,872	18,259	18,592	18,889
(Domestic civilian labor force)	16,774	17,070	17,371	17,639	17,910
Total civilian employment	15,249	15,239	15,231	15,368	15,457
Agriculture	9,537	9,529	9,520	9,512	9,481
Industry	1,826	1,794	1,771	1,822	1,851
Mining and quarrying	120	123	124	126	121
Manufacturing	1,610	1,572	1,548	1,594	1,620
Electricity, water and gas	97	100	99	102	110
Construction	562	578	581	582	584
Transportation, storage and communications	501	492	480	491	497
Wholesale and retail trade	646	637	628	656	672
Banking, insurance and real estate	204	208	211	214	216
Services	1,700	1,727	1,767	1,818	1,882
Unspecified	273	273	273	273	273
Urban and rural unemployment (excluding agricultural labor surplus)	1,525	1,831	2,140	2,271	2,453
Agricultural labor surplus at peak season /1	720	700	700	700	665
Domestic labor surplus	2,245	2,531	2,840	2,971	3,118
Domestic labor surplus ratio	13.4	14.8	16.4	16.8	17.4
Labor stock abroad	751	802	888	953	979
Total labor surplus	2,996	3,333	3,728	3,924	4,097
Total labor surplus ratio	17.1	18.6	20.4	21.1	21.7

/1 Appears also as part of employment in agriculture

Source: State Planning Organization

Table 54.

WORKERS ABROAD
(thousand)

	1981	1982
Australia	16	15
Austria	30	30
Belgium	23	25
France	50	64
Germany, Federal Republic	576	653
Libya	62	80
Netherlands	62	70
Saudi Arabia	60	80
Switzerland	22	24
Total (incl. others)	**935**	**1,064**

Source: Middle East and North Africa 1983.

TRANSPORTATION & COMMUNICATIONS

Table 55.

INFRASTRUCTURE

Km of road (1982):	60,671
	54,318 (hard surfaced)
(000 vehicles)	
Passenger cars	795.2
Trucks	397.4
Buses	105.8
Km of railroad (1982):	8,141
Passenger-km (mn)	5,488
Net ton-km (mn)	6,279

List of ports: (in order of tonnage capacity)

- Istanbul
- Izmir
- Samsun
- Mersin
- Iskenderum
- Trabzon

Telephones (1982):	1,501,977
Radio licences (1982):	4,404,000
TV licences (1982):	5,084,720
International Airports:	Esenboga (30 km from Ankara), Yesilkoy (25 km from Istanbul).
Number of passengers (000):	2,421
Freight (000 metric tons):	11,564

Source: MERI.

Table 56.

MAJOR DAILY NEWSPAPERS

Paper	City of Publication	Circulation	
Adalet	Ankara	174,000	
Ankara Ticaret	Ankara	100,000	
Baris	Ankara	150,000	
Cumhuriyet	Istanbul	125,000	
Gunaydin	Istanbul	357,873	suspended Dec 82
Hurriyet	Istanbul	750,000	
Hur Vatan	Ankara	165,000	
Milliyet	Istanbul	1,050,000	
Son Havadis	Istanbul	60,000	
Tasvir	Ankara	141,000	
Tercuman	Istanbul	515,000	suspended Aug 83
Turkish Daily News	Ankara	9,000	
Yeni Asir	Izmir	110,000	
Yenigun	Ankara	135,000	
Yeni Konya	Konya	70,000	
Yeni Meram	Konya	41,300	
Yeni Nesil	Istanbul	450,000	
Yeni Tanin	Ankara	300,000	

Source: Middle East and North Africa 1983-84

HEALTH, EDUCATION AND WELFARE

Table 57.

MEDICAL INSTITUTIONS AND PHARMACIES

	1977	1978	1979	1980	1981
In-patient institutions					
Total	772	776	822	827	831
Hospitals /1	498	497	532	536	544
Health centers	274	279	290	291	287
Out-patient institutions					
Total	7172	7481	9579	9044	9757
Government physicians	249	249	249	242	314
Dispensaries & infirmaries	35	24	20	20	20
Health units	1319	1365	1764	1827	1838
Health houses	4276	4691	6565	6594	6624
Dispensaries /2	320	320	326	326	326
Maternity & child health					
Centers	66	62	63	62	62
Branches	85	69	68	63	63
Dispensaries	36	63	63	65	65
Stations	786	638	461	445	445
Pharmacies	5878	6193	6174	6335	6914

/1 Covers non-military public and private hospitals

/2 Includes in-patient dispensaries and dispensaries attached to local governments, municipalities, associations, work places and foreign organizations.

Source: Ministry of Health and Social Welfare

Table 58.

TEACHERS AND ENROLLMENT OF PUBLIC AND PRIVATE EDUCATIONAL INSTITUTIONS

Educational Institution		1976-77	1977-78	1978-79	1079-80	1980-81
Primary School	A	42,869	43,243	43,979	44,296	45,660
	B	182,679	184,512	187,764	199,245	215,459
	C	5,503	5,458	5,575	5,622	5,695
Junior High School	A	3,067	3,317	3,600	4,103	4,314
	B	29,963	32,056	31,213	30,930	35,979
	C	1,074	1,107	1,110	1,180	1,148
High School	A	927	984	1,044	1,108	1,166
	B	29,213	30,941	33,301	36,198	41,267
	C	429	457	482	532	534
Vocational and Technical School	A	1,399	1,558	1,601	1,719	1,856
	B	23,233	24,683	25,851	28,599	33,967
	C	436	469	483	515	520

A School
B Teacher
C Enrollment (thousand)

Source: State Institute of Statistics Statistical Yearbook 1982

Table 59.

TEACHING STAFF, ENROLLMENT AND GRADUATES IN HIGHER EDUCATIONAL INSTITUTIONS

Educational Institution		1976-77	1977-78	1978-79	1979-80	1980-81
Total of Faculties	A	92	96	121	155	165
	B	10,207	11,073	12,304	14,861	15,502
	C	102,433	108,216	124,577	167,848	165,647
	D	11,253	13,656	17,919	21,703	--
Ankara University	A	12	12	12	12	12
	B	1,893	1,986	2,006	2,225	2,310
	C	16,039	17,209	19,288	19,210	19,539
	D	1,949	2,018	2,431	2,186	--
Middle East Technical University	A	5	5	5	5	5
	B	824	901	1,065	1,081	1,148
	C	9,966	10,549	11,420	11,723	11,711
	D	1,125	975	1,082	1,273	--
Hacettepe University	A	12	12	12	12	8
	B	1,501	1,656	1,845	1,897	1,491
	C	8,805	9,506	10,901	12,245	9,830
	D	704	969	1,288	1,207	--
Istanbul University	A	13	13	13	15	15
	B	2,027	2,229	2,367	2,395	2,483
	C	30,681	30,663	30,269	30,918	31,002
	D	3,115	3,189	3,036	3,305	--

A=Faculties C=Enrollment
B=Teaching Staff D=Graduates

Source: State Institute of Statistics Yearbook 1982

TEACHING STAFF, ENROLLMENT AND GRADUATES IN HIGHER EDUCATIONAL INSTITUTIONS

Educational Institution		1976-77	1977-78	1978-79	1979-80	1980-81
Istanbul Technical University	A	9	9	10	11	12
	B	760	822	818	862	912
	C	7,834	8,207	9,032	9,621	9,526
	D	700	807	727	1,307	--
Bogazici University	A	3	3	3	3	3
	B	184	191	200	233	229
	C	1,807	2,283	2,500	2,462	2,530
	D	366	475	482	400	--
Ege University	A	8	8	17	17	17
	B	1,218	1,347	1,767	1,910	1,853
	C	11,922	11,840	13,523	14,697	15,015
	D	1,784	2,522	2,435	1,785	--
Ataturk Univesity	A	8	8	8	8	7
	B	655	675	716	724	712
	C	7,380	7,345	8,920	6,589	5,991
	D	536	680	1,129	1,264	--
Karadeniz Technical University	A	5	5	5	5	5
	B	319	287	309	292	285
	C	2,992	2,886	2,742	2,646	2,558
	D	791	520	427	303	--

For Product Safety Concerns and Information please contact our EU representative GPSR@taylorandfrancis.com
Taylor & Francis Verlag GmbH, Kaufingerstraße 24, 80331 München, Germany

www.ingramcontent.com/pod-product-compliance
Ingram Content Group UK Ltd.
Pitfield, Milton Keynes, MK11 3LW, UK
UKHW022125190926
475702UK00013B/1661
9781138902268